unter

More than conquerors

CESAR & CLAUDIA CASTELLANOS

post-encounter

POST-ENCOUNTER
FOR MEN

Cesar Castellanos D.© 2003

Published by G12 Editors

ventas@g12bookstore.com

sales@g12bookstore.com

www.g12bookstore.com

ISBN 1-932285-38-5

All rights reserved. Copyright©2003

The total or partial reproduction of
this book is forbidden under any
of its forms, neither graphic,
electronic or audiovisual, without
previous written authorization
from publishers.

Impreso en Colombia
Printed in Colombia

CONTENTS

CONTENTS

I have had the opportunity of attending many Encounters, which are three-day retreats. There I have been able to observe in the countenance of many, the reflection of the oppression the enemy has exercised upon them. However, the marvelous work that God performs, despite the short duration of the Encounter, can be described as something miraculous. When we see the joy that emulates through their lives, as they hug their family, friends and leaders, we become compelled to give thanks to God, for how He has transformed their lives in a supernatural manner.

The Encounter could be compared to the exodus of the people of Israel from the land of Egypt under the leadership of Moses. God did this to liberate His people from the oppressive rule of Pharaoh. The only request the Lord presented to Pharaoh was: "Let my people go for three days, so that they may serve me in the wilderness." The Egyptian King understood that this was the appointed time for the people to be made free and for this reason his heart was hardened and he didn't let them go. God drastically intervened and Pharaoh could not find any other option than to permit their liberation. When they felt what it was like to be free, great joy came upon the people, but Pharaoh hardened his heart towards them and lanced a counter-attack with the intention of destroying them. He desired for them die by drowning in the sea.

While Moses interceded for the people, God told him: "Why do you cry out to me? Tell the people to march". He extended his staff and the Red Sea that was in front of them divided in two, so that the people could cross, walking on dry ground. God, through His immense power, opened the sea so that the people could have an exit, escaping from the hands of the enemy.

I find a great parallel between the people of Israel and what they went through and the people that begin to establish themselves in the vision. The Encounter signifies freedom. It signifies leaving the oppression of Egypt. However, after this great liberation comes a counter-attack of the enemy where he attempts to seduce the people again, so that they may go back and return to the slavery of sin once again. Yet, just as God opened the waters of the Red Sea, he has also opened a breech, so that His people may cross victoriously.

If we sought for a definition to describe what the Post-encounter is, we could say: "The Post-encounter is the way traced by God, for His people to advance after Him while not being detained by adversities."
The objective of each of these teachings is, to help those who come to an Encounter, to secure the deliverance that they have received and the blessings that were given by God.

The Apostle Peter said: "Be sober, be vigilant; because your adversary the Devil walks about like a roaring lion, seeking whom he may devour. Resist him, steadfast in the faith." (I Peter 5: 8-9a). If each one who assists in the Encounter and makes the effort to continue faithfully in the Post-encounter process, God will count them in as His people and will bless them in a great way.

Saul of Tarsus' success was based on him being Jewish and having been educated by one of the best bible teachers like Gamaliel. He was also known for being a Roman citizen who defended his traditions with great zeal. But when he had his first encounter with Jesus, he understood that he had worked towards the wrong type of success. This encounter was so powerful that he later said, "But whatever things were gain to me, those things I have counted as loss for the sake of Christ. More than that, I count all things to be loss in view of the surpassing value of knowing Christ Jesus my Lord, for whom I have suffered the loss of all things, and count them but rubbish so that I may gain Christ." Philippians 3:7-8 (NASU).

Saul went away to Damascus for three days to think, introspect, repent and meditate. Scripture took on a new life form. The revelation of the Messiah became so clear to him, that from that moment onward, he purposed in his heart, to dedicate his life and every part of his being to the service of the Lord Jesus. What is so impressive about Saul is that after his encounter, wherever he went, he never ceased preaching Jesus and never considered the consequences that he labored to take the message of Jesus Christ to the ends of the earth.

Cesar Castellanos D.

Acts 9:4-22

CORRESPONDING
BIBLICAL
FOUNDATION

I John 2:27

Exodus 14:15

Galatians 2:18

Ephesians 4:22-32

Isaiah 53:4-5

Be firm in your Decisions

1

THE CONVERSION

Without a doubt, Saul came to be one of the most important figures of Christianity throughout all the ages because of his firm determination of serving Jesus with all his heart. His conversion was supernatural. He received a heavenly vision, which permitted him to continue the mission started by Jesus who was that of discipling the whole nations.

Saul was confronted with his past (Acts 9:4-5).

To the Lord's question, "Why do you persecute me?" and knowing the life that Saul lived, his answer could have been very simple, if he had the strength to answer: "Because the zeal for tradition consumes me." With the powerful experience that Saul had when Jesus revealed himself to him, his whole theology was left without foundation. For the first time, he felt unable to hold on to that which had been his hope in the past.

He received a revelation of his own nature (Verse 6).

He was trembling and scared. When God confronts us, the hidden things in our hearts come out into the light and we feel ashamed, for we see our own nature clearly, feeling weak and impotent before his Majesty. This scares us and makes us tremble because no one can stand in His presence.

He had his first encounter (Verse 9).

For three days he had intimacy with God. During this time he had no desire to eat nor drink, all he yearned for was to pray.

A prophet prayed for him (Verse 17).

He received his vision and the infilling of the Holy Spirit in that encounter.

He made the decision of being baptized (Verse 18).

Saul, a man knowledgeable in the law, knew that God was a God of covenant. The way in which God would relate to his people would be through the covenant of baptism, which represents death on the cross.

He spent time being discipled (Verse 19).

The time he spent sharing with Christian leaders gave him the foundation to be able to develop the ministry God had entrusted him with.

Saul preached diligently about Jesus Christ (Verse 20).

Saul's conversion was something that caught the attention of those that knew of his religious zeal and they were amazed that he converted to Christianity.

Saul made a real effort (Verse 22).

It is imperative that everyone who has had a genuine encounter with Jesus makes a real effort to share the love of Jesus with others. Later on, Paul said, "For I am not ashamed of the gospel of Christ, for it is the power of God to salvation for everyone who believes." Now that you have attended an encounter, it is important that you make it evident to others; be it your family, your co-workers or your neighbors. You should share with each one of them your personal experience of how and when you accepted Jesus. Doing this is very important, for it helps us to keep or maintain a good testimony before them.

He believed Jesus was the Christ.

Although Saul knew the biblical prophesies regarding the Messiah, these were not revealed to him until he had his encounter with Jesus. His personal experience led him to understand the biblical teaching. On this issue, John says that this same anointing teaches us all things (I John 2:27).

One of the strategies the enemy uses after an encounter, when deep and intimate experiences with God have taken place, is to prepare a heavy attack that is cunning and quick. Its purpose is to rob you of everything you received from God during those days. We must understand that it is hard for Satan to accept the fact that those who were once his slaves are now experiencing the freedom of the Christian life and he will try, by all means possible, to cool off your relationship with God. To do this, he will use things that you have desired in the past but were not able to attain, for example: lucrative but illicit business deals, a sudden meeting with a woman who was previously uninterested in you, a raise in salary at work which now demands more of the time which you were dedicating to serving God, etc.

Some students performed an experiment once: they placed a frog in a container with water and they started to slowly heat the water. The water finally reached the boiling point but the frog never tried to jump out. Why? Because the changes in the environment were so subtle that the frog didn't realize it until it was too late. It is so important to maintain for our spiritual eyes to be alert at all times to avoid falling into the enemy's trap.

When Moses saw Pharaoh's army coming towards them with the intention of destroying them, which was after they had successfully left Egypt in victory, he threw himself on the ground and called out to God. And the Lord said to him, "Why do you cry to me? Tell the children of Israel to go forward," (Exodus 14:15).

TRY NOT TO GET INVOLVED WITH THE PAST AGAIN

Paul said, "For if I rebuild what I have once destroyed, I prove myself to be a transgressor" (Galatians 2:18 NASU).

I had just started my Christian life and found out that a cousin had become a Christian. One day we met at a family reunion and what a surprise it was for me to see him drinking alcohol just like the rest of the unbelievers.

This saddened my heart so much, that I asked him why he was doing it, to which he answered, "I want to enjoy life but before I die, I'll repent." I told him, "You don't know how much longer you're going to live!" Although I tried to reconcile him with God, it was of to no avail.

Two months later this young man drowned without getting a second chance. He was the light of salvation for his whole family but he got trapped by getting involved with the past. We should understand that within us there exists a nature that tries to rebel against God in order to make us slaves to our own desires and passions.

Our carnal nature is as dangerous as a trained feline that only needs to taste a single drop of blood to revive its savage instincts and cause it to rise up against his masters. Paul said in Ephesians 4:22-32:

1. Put off the old man, which is addicted to deceitful lusts. To be addicted means "to cling to destructive habits". And the only way to be free is by renewing our mind through the Word of God, which will produce holiness within us.

2. Therefore, putting away lying, speak truth to your neighbor. Bad company corrupts good character. Lies do not come from God.

3. Be angry but do not sin. Do not let the sun go down on your wrath. Solomon said that anger rests in the heart of fools, but a gentle answer turns away wrath.

4. Don't give way to the devil. A person who is easily angered and resentful opens a door for the enemy and he will no longer attack from the outside but from the inside.

5. Let him who stole, steal no longer, but rather let him labor, working with his hands that which is good, that he may have something to give to those in need. Whoever had the habit of stealing must now make up for it by being generous.

6. Let no corrupt word proceed out of your mouth, but only that, which is good for edification, that it may impart grace to the hearers.

All negative words or complaints become like a contaminated river. When Israel wanted to drink water in the desert, they could not because the waters were bitter. But as they threw the tree into the water as God had instructed them, the water became sweet and the poison disappeared. In the same manner, if the tree of the cross is in our life, then every word that comes out of our lips will be a spring of living water.

7. And do not grieve the Holy Spirit of God, by whom you were sealed for the day of redemption. The Holy Spirit has come to live in your life, but He doesn't want to be treated as if He didn't exist. Spiritual indifference makes Him sad and His blessings can disappear because of this.

8. Put away from you all bitterness, wrath, anger, clamor, evil speaking and all malice. And be kind to one another, tenderhearted, forgiving one another even as God in Christ forgave you.

CONCLUSION

As you can see, we are the ones that need to put off those things, which can become obstacles for our spiritual development. There are areas in our lives where God does not intervene. He did his part by taking our sicknesses and pain upon his body on the cross. He took our rebellions and our sins and that is why He was crushed and punished; but his wounds became our deliverance and our medicine. (Isaiah 53:4-5). Although the spirit of rebellion has already been taken away through the cross of Calvary, we should make an effort to free ourselves of those habits that kept us bound to a past in misery because of wickedness and renew our intimacy with God and His Word daily.

APPLICATION

Decide today to make a definite break from your past and start living your life in blessing (the teacher should say a prayer for this).

1   Questionnaire for further study

1. Now that you have had a genuine encounter with Jesus, list at least 3 determining aspects which you know will positively change your life. _____

_____
_____
_____
_____.

2. Through which concrete actions will your family, friends, co-workers, and acquaintances know Jesus in you. _____

_____
_____
_____.

3. Why should you avoid attitudes and habits from your past life?

_____
_____
_____
_____.

4. Make a commitment with God and yourself concerning the following aspects:

LIE:_____

_____
_____.

ANGER:_____

_____
_____.

VOCABULARY:_____

_____
_____.

Psalm 16:11

CORRESPONDING
BIBLICAL
FOUNDATION

Relating to God

Psalm 100:2-4

Jonah 2:9-10

Colossians 3:15-17

I Thessalonians 5:16-19

Matthew 12:36-37

Mark 11:24

Romans 8:32

John 14:13-14

2

LESSON

I Timothy 2:5

Philippians 4:19

2 Corinthians 1:20

I John 5:14

WE NEED TO RELATE
PERSONALLY WITH GOD

My life was so impacted by Claudia when I met her that I had no doubt that she would be my wife. One of my greatest desires was to be with her. There was no greater commitment than to be by her side. I was willing to make any necessary change in my schedule to spend time with the woman that would make my heart vibrate. If someone had told me, "Don't go see Claudia because it's pretty boring," I would have answered, "It's exciting to be with her! When I'm with Claudia I want time to stop. She makes me feel important and valued. Since it is hard to express love with just words, I want to spend every second of my day with her."

Something similar happens in our relationship with God. Just as unique as the experience of love, so is the experience of prayer. Only he who practices it can live it. Talking with God can never be boring, for each second that He allows us to be in His presence is the most powerful experience, almost indescribable. We don't want that time to ever stop, for there is nothing more important than being in His presence. He makes us feel important. He shows us his love. He reveals his will to us. He protects us under his shadow and provides for all of our needs.

The only way prayer can become monotonous and boring is when it lacks love and commitment. Have you ever experienced showing love and it not being returned to you? That is how God feels because He has shown us his love in so many ways and yet He still sees how some of his children keep a distance with an attitude of indifference.
I have been praying for more than thirty years and I can guarantee you there is nothing more exciting and noble than to be in His presence.

The psalmist said, "In your presence is fullness of joy, at your right hand are pleasures forevermore," (Psalm 16:11). During all these years I have been able to relate personally to God. He is as real as the people around us whom we love. If we can love those whom we see, we will also be able to love that God whom we don't see.

UNDERSTANDING WHAT A DEVOTIONAL IS

The way we relate to God is through prayer. In order to develop this very important habit, we need to dedicate some time to it everyday, alone and in intimacy with God, which is called devotional time. This is a time where we can express to Him what is in our hearts and where He will reveal his will to us and will show his great love toward us. In order for your devotional to be effective we suggest for you to:
   - Choose the hour and length of time for your devotional.
   - Have privacy.
   - Get into the habit of doing it in the morning, before starting your daily activities.
   - Be honest with yourself and with God.
   - Have your Bible on hand, along with a notebook and write down whatever God talks to you through his Word.
   - Have a list of the requests you will present to the Lord in prayer.

A. Entering into His presence

We must understand that within us there are two natures, the spiritual one and the carnal one. Paul said the desire of the flesh is against the spirit and the desire of the spirit is against the flesh. That is why in order to enter into communion with God there is an internal struggle. Besides, the mind tries to deviate constantly. The more that we practice praying, our spirit man will get stronger and the carnal nature will weaker.

B. Starting to pray joyfully,
with Thanksgiving

"Come before Him with joyful songs... Enter His gates with thanksgiving, and into His courts with praise; be thankful to Him, and bless His name," (Psalm 100:2,4).
There is no greater joy than being able to be in the presence of our God.
The attitude of our hearts determines the successes we will have in our prayers. To be able to persevere in prayer we should be always joyful.
A person with a thankful heart is the one that recognizes the word of God in each aspect of his life. The doors that will take us to the castle of His Majesty are called "thankfulness".

Think about everything, which you should give thanks to God for. While Dr. Norman Vincent Peele counseled a bitter man, he told him, "Get up and walk around this room and make a list of everything that gives you enthusiasm." This man walked around for a while and finally said, "I don't see anything." "For sure you're nearsighted. What are those two things you're walking on?" "Oh, of course, they're my feet..." "How would you be if you only had one, or none at all?" (The persistent optimist, page 127). That man was able to recognize that there are many things, which we can give thanks to God for.

Only one of the ten was grateful.

Gratitude is one of the most important ways to express our love to God and to maintain a tight relationship with Him. You may possibly remember that scene where the Lord healed ten lepers and only one of them returned to give Him thanks; therefore, the Lord asked him, "Were there not ten cleansed? Where are the nine?" Only one out of the ten had the correct attitude of gratitude and

he was not a Jew but a Samaritan. Paul said, "Not that
I seek the gift, but I seek the fruit that abounds to your
account." We express our gratitude through attitudes
or emotions, and there should always be a verbal
expression on our lips.

He was freed because he gave thanks.

God had given Jonah the mission of preaching in the
city of Nineveh, but he didn't want them to get saved;
rather that the judgment of God reaches them. This
is why he ran from the presence of God and ended up
in the belly of a large fish. Being in the dark belly of
the fish, he was able to acknowledge his sin, repent
and made a commitment saying, "But I, with a song of
thanksgiving, will sacrifice to you. What I have vowed I
will make good. Salvation comes from the Lord. And the
Lord commanded the fish, and it vomited Jonah onto dry
land," (Jonah 2:9-10 NIV).

Whoever departs from the divine purpose, will find
himself in a situation similar to Jonah who, because he
fled from God, his life was going downhill until he reached
the depth of the ocean, where he felt he was losing all
hope of life. But God had prepared a large fish, which
became Jonah's salvation. Not until Jonah opened his
mouth in gratitude towards God did the Lord order the
fish to vomit him onto dry land.

Gratitude should flow out of our hearts at all times,
in good times and in bad times, because we know that
everything works together for our good. The apostle
Paul said, "In everything give thanks for this is the will of
God in Christ Jesus for you."

God has contact with thankful believers.

"And whatever you do in word or deed, do all in the name of
the Lord Jesus, giving THANKS to God the Father through
Him," (Colossians 3:17).

"Pray without ceasing, in everything give thanks for this is the will of God in Christ Jesus for you. Do not quench the Spirit," (I Thessalonians 5:16-19).

Prayer and thanksgiving should remain together. As we develop them and make them part of our personality, we will be fulfilling God's will and we will be keeping alive the flame of revival. The best medicine for bitterness, pain and failure is giving thanks.

The door to reach the presence of God is called "thanksgiving".
No one can enjoy the presence of the Father until thanksgiving is overflowing from their heart.
Although we yearn for the presence of God and His power, we will not see it in its fullness until we learn to give thanks, in whatever situation. The divine presence will not be present until we open our mouth to give thanks. Thanksgiving generates praise, and this moves us to worship the Lord permanently for all the undeserved favors we have obtained from his loving hand (Psalm 100:4-5).

The Lord said, "But I say unto you that for every idle word men may speak, they will give account of it in the Day of Judgment. For by your words you will be justified, and by your words you will be condemned" (Matthew 12:36-37).

There is a great power residing in this small member, the tongue, to such a point that your salvation or your condemnation depends on this member. Your tongue can lead you to complain or can motivate you to praise. According to the Greek, when Scripture says, "for every idle word," the word idle has a connotation of "empty word, that gives no fruit." For every empty word that man may speak, he will give account on the final day.

JESUS TAUGHT HIS DISCIPLES
HOW TO PRAY

The Lord never taught his disciples how to preach but He did make special time to teach them how to pray. He gathered them together and told them, "...you will pray like this..." and He gave them clear instructions on how the prayer should be developed so that prayer would be effective. If you are a disciple of Christ, you need to learn how to communicate with God.

Prayer is the key that puts us in contact with God.

When you arrive home, you usually have the right key so you can go in. There is only one way through which you can communicate with God, and that is through prayer. That is the master key that opens the door so we can be in direct contact with God.

Prayer is a personal relationship with God, where He delights himself hearing each word that comes out of our lips. "Therefore I say unto you, whatever things you ask when you pray, believe that you receive them, and you will have them," (Mark 11:24).

The Lord wants us to enjoy his intimacy, in the same manner that a loving father enjoys his relationship with his kids. He is willing to move his angels in our favor so that we may obtain what our heart desires; because if we are able to ask in faith, He will do it. "He that did not spare His own Son, but delivered Him up for us all, how shall He not with Him also freely give us all things?" (Romans 8:32).

A few years ago my wife and I started praying so we could have a 15-minute radio program. She said to me, "Why are you going to pray for a 15-minute radio program? Let's pray for a 1-hour one." That's what we did. Later she told me, "Why don't we pray for the Lord to give us a whole evening?" And I answered her, "Let's pray all night long", she then added, "Why don't we pray for a radio station?" And I said to her, "Alright, let's pray for a radio station." We started praying for the radio station and we said, "Lord, we would like you to give us the radio station before the end of this year." God always answers prayer and before the year was up we had the radio station.

Ask in the Name of Jesus.

"And whatever you ask in My name, that I will do, that the Father may be glorified in the Son. If you ask anything in My name, I will do it"
(John 14:13-14).

Scripture does not teach us that we cannot go directly to God the Father. Any prayer you lift up has to be directed to the Father, in the name of Jesus.

God is Holy, extremely Holy and He does not allow, accepts, nor participates in anybody's sin. His holiness maintains Him completely away from all type of impurity and everything that surrounds Him is also holy and proclaims His marvelous works.

Jesus is our only mediator.

When God wanted to have a relationship with Israel, He did not stand for their complaints or their murmurings. That is why He chose Moses to be the intermediary between them and God. "For there is one God and one Mediator between God and men, the Man Christ Jesus," (I Timothy 2:5). When you direct yourself to God, you should do so in the name of Jesus. When you do so, he becomes a bridge between you and God.

Your prayer can be, "Lord, I come before you in the name of Jesus of Nazareth and I present these needs to you........... (specify each one of them), trusting that I will receive them through your divine grace."

When one uses the name of Jesus, He is ready to answer each one of your requests. It doesn't take many years in Christianity for the Lord to answer prayers. The only thing He requires is that we ask in faith and in the name of Jesus.

Jesus is our provider.

God is Lord of everything. In Him there is abundance and He is always generous with each of his kids. His goodness is unlimited, his favors are unlimited and you can start to enjoy all the blessings that He has reserved for each one of us.

"My God shall supply all your needs according to his riches in glory through Christ Jesus," (Philippians 4:19).

Jesus said yes to his promises.

"For all the promises of God in Him (in Jesus Christ) are yes, and in Him amen, to the glory of God through us," (II Corinthians 1:20).

God himself makes sure that everything He promises gets fulfilled. If God promised to provide all our needs and He said, "I do it," He will do it. We should answer, "Amen, Lord, I am totally sure that I will obtain each one of the requests I have presented to you, through your grace and your mercy."

HAVE YOUR BOOK OF DREAMS

My wife and I, have developed the habit of writing down our requests. We still have a notebook we used in our devotional time in the year 1983, where we wrote our requests with the date we prayed and the date that we received the answer.

In that same year the Lord answered 70% of everything we asked of Him during that year, including financial provision and the salvation of relatives. The Lord is pleased when in prayer we describe our request with details or even if we use graphics. Our daughters have learned this principle. Each one of them has their own notebook and they call it, "Book of Dreams". In it they write in detail everything they desire. They download from the internet many of the images of what they desire and they glue them to their notebook.

The Lord always answers them; many times much faster than what they expect. "Now this is the confidence that we have in Him, that if we ask anything according to His will, He hears us," (I John 5:14).

CONCLUSION

Without a doubt, having a personal relationship with God is a fountain of life. Make the decision and start this new stage, following these simple steps, which will give you a successful and full life, allowing you to experience God's greatness in your life.

APPLICATION

Start right tomorrow your time of devotions and experience God's wonders in your life.

2   Questionnaire for further study

1. Explain in your own words, "What is a devotional?"

_____

_____

_____ .

2. To strengthen your relationship with God, as of today establish for your devotional the following:
PLACE:_____TIME:_____A.M.

3. List at least 3 aspects you take into account when doing your devotional:_____

_____

_____ .

4. Briefly write your personal experience in your devotional concerning the following aspects:

ENTERING IN HIS PRESENCE _____

_____

_____ .

GIVE THANKS_____

_____

_____ .

ASK IN THE NAME OF JESUS _____

_____

_____ .

5. Why is prayer the key to relate with God?

_____

_____

_____ .

6. Start to make your own DREAM BOOK

Exodus 20:4-5
John 4:24

CORRESPONDING
BIBLICAL
FOUNDATION

The power of
Worship and Praise

I Kings 8:27
Psalm 95:6
Philippians 2:9-11
Revelation 4:9-11
Psalm 143:6
Exodus 17:8-16
Psalm 34
Job 38:7
Matthew 12:35-37
James 3:7-9
Hebrews 13:15
Psalm 154:2
Psalm 111:1
Psalm 47:7
Psalm 63:4
Psalm 150:4
Psalm 148:11-14
Hebrews 11:3
2 Timothy 3:16
2 Peter 1:21
John 20:30-31
Romans 10:17
Hebrews 4:12
Colossians 3:16
I Peter 2:1-2
Ephesians 4:31
Matthew 4:4
Hebrews 5:12-14

LESSON

WORSHIP

Man was created to worship God. When Satan saw the intimate communion that man enjoyed with his Creator, he was full of envy and wanted to destroy that relationship and channel that human need for his own benefit so man would bow down to him. Cunningly, he sold him the idea that if he ate of the forbidden fruit, he would be like God. Satan knew that if man accepted this offer, he would be completely separated from God and would enter into Satan's territory, being under his dominion, since the only thing that separates man from God is sin.

When Satan tempted the Lord, one of his offers was, "All these things I will give You if You will fall down and worship me." And the Lord answered, "Away with you, Satan! For it is written, 'You will worship the Lord your God, and Him only will you serve'" (Matthew 4:10).

So then we can notice that the Lord tells the adversary that worship belongs exclusively to God and cannot be given to anyone else. Neither can we give worship to any object, symbol or image. Worship belongs only and exclusively to God and no one else.

In the Ten Commandments the Lord himself taught that one of the reasons why divine judgment comes upon humanity is because of worshiping images because these lift up a great barrier between God and man (Exodus 20:4-5). To worship what is not God, calls God's wrath up to the fourth generation.

God is Spirit and the only way to worship him is in spirit. The Lord taught, "God is spirit; and those who worship Him must worship in spirit and in truth," (John 4:24).

HOW CAN WE WORSHIP GOD

A skeptic professor once asked a small boy, "Tell me, where is God?" And the boy told him, "I'll ask you another question. Tell me, where isn't God?" We know His presence fills the heavens and all the earth. Solomon, in the dedication of the temple said, "But will God really dwell on the earth? The heavens, even the highest heaven, cannot contain you. How much less this temple?" (I Kings 8:27). We can all feel God's presence wherever we are, even though there are some places that seem more appropriate than others, that inspire and attract the presence of God more. He can hear our prayers, no matter where we are.

Only through the Bible can we learn the correct way of how to worship God. The Lord teaches us guidelines that will help us understand what worship is.

To kneel down.

"Come, let us bow down in worship, let us kneel before the Lord our Maker..." (Psalm 95:6).
The words "kneel" and "knee" have the same meaning in Hebrew, which is, "blessing". When you kneel, you are blessing the name of God.

The apostle Paul said, referring to Jesus after his victory over death, "Therefore God exalted him to the highest place and gave him the name that is above every name, that at the name of Jesus every knee should bow, in heaven and on earth and under the earth, and every tongue confess that Jesus Christ is Lord, to the glory of God the Father," (Philippians 2:9-11).

To bow down.

"Come, let us bow down in worship, let us kneel before the Lord our Maker," (Psalm 95:6).
When the people would bow down, they would cover their face before the presence of God. This is an expression of brokenness, humility and of rendering. When the Jews would worship God, they would always do so with their face to the ground. They would bow their heads, placing it on the ground before the presence of God.

In Revelation the apostle John saw the angelical worship and said, "Whenever the living creatures give glory, honor and thanks to Him that sits on the throne and who lives forever and ever, the twenty-four elders fall down before him who sits on the throne, and worship him who lives forever and ever. They lay their crowns before the throne and say: 'You are worthy, our Lord and God, to receive glory and honor and power, for you created all things, and by your will they were created and have their being," (Revelation 4:9-11).

The twenty-four elders are a representation of the twelve patriarchs of Israel and of the twelve apostles; who at the moment of worship, bow down before the Lord, worship him, give him their crowns and acknowledge his authority.

God gave the prophet Isaiah the revelation of His glory saying, "In the year that King Uzziah died, I saw the Lord seated on the throne, high and exalted, and the train of his robe filled the temple. Above him were seraphs, each with six wings: with two wings they covered their faces, with two they covered their feet, and with two were flying. And they were calling to one another: "Holy, holy, holy is the Lord almighty; the whole earth is full of His glory" (Isaiah 6:1-3).

When God revealed himself to the prophet, His presence was with seraphs ("seraph" means "fire").

These angelic beings dwell very close to God and they represent the glorious and powerful fire of the Lord. Each one had six wings. With two they covered their face, with two they covered their feet and with two they would fly. To cover their face symbolized worship. They humble themselves before the Majesty of the one who sits on the throne and they express that they depend solely on Him. To cover their feet symbolizes renouncing to all impurity in our daily walk.

The Lord told Moses, "Take off your sandals, for the place where you are standing is holy ground." The seraphs utilized four of their wings to worship God and with the other two they would fly. To fly symbolizes their service to their King. Throughout this passage, we understand that for God, worship comes before service. There are many believers who have a beautiful spirit of service. They like to serve but they spend very little time in worship, which brings people into the presence of God.

God is Spirit

He has always existed. He created all things, visible and invisible. The only one who knows Him and has made Him known to us is the Lord Jesus. He was the one who taught us that the only way to worship a God who is spirit needs to be of the same spiritual nature; and the only ones who possess that are those who have been born again (John 3:3). We don't worship any god, we worship the God who created heaven, who created the earth, who created the universe, the Creator of each life, the God who sent his son Jesus Christ to save us.

To spread out hands.

"I spread out my hands to you; my soul thirsts for you like a parched land," (Psalm 143:6).
To spread out your hands is a symbol of rendering and, when we do so, we're telling God we depend solely on Him.

In Exodus 17:8-16, Scripture tells us a story about when Israel was in battle against Amalek. God told them that Moses' arms should not go down until they obtained the victory. When Moses had his hands up high, God's armies helped Israel's army in the battle and they started defeating the Amaleks but when Moses' arms got tired, the angels no longer fought along side them for they needed Moses' arms to be on high so they could act.

That is why, Aaron and Hur each took one of Moses' arms and held them. This way, the Israelites were able to prevail against Amalek and defeat them.

This teaches us that when we lift up our hands on high, those diabolic powers fighting against us are broken, overcome and put to shame because God's army starts to work through us and for us.

PRAISE

"I will bless the Lord at all time; His praise will always be on my lips. My soul will boast in the Lord; let the afflicted hear and rejoice. Glorify the Lord with me; let us exalt His name together," (Psalm 34:1-3).

"In the beginning God created the heavens and the earth," (Genesis 1:1). Before everything existed, God already was. He created all things and one of those things was music. This is not the adversary's invention. Music is God's creation. It was given as a means for the angels to praise Him. Praise existed, even before the world was created.

Who worshiped God while He founded the earth? All the stars of the morning did so and all the beings created by God rejoiced. Praise produces a great spiritual joy. The Psalmist said, "Yet you are enthroned as the Holy One; you are the praise of Israel" (Psalm 22:3).

If the people praise God, God will be in the midst of them.

The power of man's life is specifically centered in the tongue; his well being on earth and his security in the life to come depends on what he expresses with it. If he expresses the right and the just, the Lord Jesus said, "The good man brings good things out of the good stored up in him and the evil man brings evil things out of the evil stored up in him. But I tell you that men will have to give account on the Day of Judgment for every careless word they have spoken. For by your words you will be acquitted, by your words you will be condemned," (Matthew 12:35-37).

The good man is the one who knows how to discern his words; he understands that these are a result of what he has allowed in his thoughts, for once they enter the mind, they are set in the heart; and we speak what is in our heart. On the last day man will have to give an account for every word pronounced that is not for edification and words that do not bear fruit; since our words are what save us or condemn us.

Although the tongue is one of the smallest members of our body, nevertheless it decides where we will spend eternity. "But no man can tame the tongue. It is a restless evil, full of deadly poison. With the tongue we praise our Lord and Father, and with it we curse men, who have been made in God's likeness," (James 3:8-9).

Although man has conquered outer space by sending satellites to different planets, he has yet to be able to control his tongue. Only with Jesus' help will we be able to have dominion over every word that we speak. We are aware that as believers we have to resist our enemy, for he opposes us praising our God.

In days of old he put his eyes on a man named Job.
Job never spoke any negative word of complaint, nor of
curse; he never slandered his neighbor; he always praised
God; with his words he would direct the lost and give
strength to the tired.
His lips were like the medicine for the sick and like the dew
to a thirsty land. Satan accused this man before God in
order to try to destroy him but Job never sinned with his
mouth nor attributed any silly thing to God.

"Through Jesus, therefore, let us continually offer to God a
sacrifice of praise, the fruit of lips that confess His name,"
(Hebrews 13:15).

A. Benefits of Praise

Praise has the power of quieting the voice of the
enemy. Psalm 8:2a says, "From the lips of children
and nursing infants you have ordained strength." The
Lord also said, "Because of your enemies, that You
may silence the enemy and the avenger."

John teaches us that the accuser of the brethren is
Satan and he accuses us before God day and night.
But when you persevere in praise, God shuts the
mouth of the accuser, keeping him quiet because the
voice of praise silences the demons.

Praise lifts up a very tall wall of protection around
your life and the life of your family, a place where the
adversary will not be able to get to. Our life is secure
because of praise. In it there is a powerful protection
from God for us, for our family and for our finances.

B. When should we Praise God?

"Everyday I will bless You, and I will praise Your name forever and ever," (Psalm 145:2).

"I will bless the Lord at all times, His praise will always be on my lips. My soul will boast in the Lord; let the afflicted hear and rejoice. Glorify the Lord with me; let us exalt His name together," (Psalm 34:1).

When should we praise the Lord? At all times, in every moment; each situation should be a reason to praise the Lord.

C. How should we Praise the Lord?

- Wholeheartedly. "I will praise the Lord with my whole heart, in the assembly of the upright and in the congregation," (Psalm 111:1).
- With understanding. "For God is the King of all the earth; sing praises with understanding," (Psalm 47:7). Understanding is the divine creativity and inspiration, where we can exalt the characteristics of God.
- Blessing His name. "Thus I will bless You while I live; I will lift up my hands in Your name," (Psalm 63:4).
- With timbrel and dance. "Praise Him with stringed instruments and flutes," (Psalm 150:4). We should praise Him with all musical instruments. Share regarding the cymbals, the timbrel, the harp and dance.

D. Who Should Praise?

"Kings of the earth and all peoples; princes and all judges of the earth; both young men and maidens; old men and children. Let them praise the name of the Lord, for His name alone is exalted; His glory is above the earth and heaven. And He has exalted the horn of his people, the praise of all his saints - of all the children of Israel, of people near to Him. Praise the Lord!" (Psalm 148:11-14)

CONCLUSION

In short, God created praise. Praise has always existed. When God created the earth, He did it in the midst of praise; the door that allows us to enter into the Lord's presence is praise; the clothing worthy to present ourselves with respectability in the eyes of God is praise.

Praise lifts up a wall of protection around our life and the life of our beloved ones. Satan was not able to pass the wall that protected Job and his family until God allowed him.

Praise is our strength; praise quiets the voice of the enemy and of the avenger; praise produces deliverance within us and those around us. Everything that exists, everything that breathes should praise the Lord.

We should praise Him everyday, at every moment, in our heart with understanding and with our lips.

APPLICATION

Dedicate some time during class to worship and praise the Lord. Motivate your students to do so until it becomes a lifestyle, expressing their gratitude this way, feeling the divine security in their lives and in the lives of their beloved ones.

3   Questionnaire for further study

1. What is worship?
_____
_____
_____.

2. What is praise?
_____
_____
_____.

3. How can we worship God according to Psalm 95:6 and Psalm 143:6?
_____
_____
_____.

4. Answer:

    a. Who praised God when He formed the earth?
    _____
    _____
    _____.

    b. When should we praise God?
    _____
    _____
    _____.

    c. How should we praise Him?
    With all_____.
    Blessing His_____.
    And_____.

d. Who should praise Him?

_____

_____

_____.

5. Assist the next intercession meeting of your ministry and share your experience:

_____

_____

_____.

BIBLICAL
FOUNDATIONAL
REFERENCE

2 Timothy 2:16

CORRESPONDING
BIBLICAL
FOUNDATION

The Bible, the book that will transform your Life

Mark 11:22

John 1:1-2

Psalm 18:13

Psalm 33:6

Hebrews 11:3

2 Peter 1:21

Isaiah 30:8

Daniel 12:4

Romans 10:17

Hebrews 4:12

Matthew 24:35

John 6:63

Isaiah 55:11

Colossians 3:16

1 Peter 2:1-2

Ephesians 4:31

Matthew 4:4

Hebrews 5:12-14

4

LESSON

THE AUTHORITY OF THE WORD

"Jesus answered saying, 'Have faith in God. For assuredly, I say unto you, whoever says to this mountain, 'Be removed and be cast into the sea', and does not doubt in his heart, but believes that those things he says will be done, he will have whatever he says. Therefore I say to you, whatever things you ask when you pray, believe that you receive them, and you will have them." (Mark 11:22)

The whole system of things in which we live, moves through the word. What we say will determine what we become and what we do; through it we plot a way of life or of death. The Lord Jesus Christ said, "For by your words you will be acquitted, by your words you will be condemned. Men will have to give account on the Day of Judgment for every careless word they have spoken."

The Lord always acts in line with the Word. Before God created the earth He said, "In the beginning was the Word and Jesus Christ is the Word, and the Word was with God, and the Word was God. He was in the beginning with God," (John 1:1,2).

When God purposed in His heart to create the world and create man, he simply sent His Word. Each word given by God is sent full of power. The word "power", in Greek, is "dunamis", which means "dynamite". "The Lord thundered from heaven, and the Most High uttered His voice..." (Psalm 18:13). Just one word from God can give life, can create or can throw down. "By the word of the Lord the heavens were made, and all the host of them by the breath of His mouth," (Psalm 33:6).

Before the angels existed, before there was a world, before there were beings, God was. And only He created the heavens and the earth through His Word. But we can only comprehend this through faith. "By faith we understand that the worlds were framed by the word of God, so that the things which are seen were not made of things which are visible," (Hebrews 11:3).

What can be seen today was created by what could not be seen. Behind this visible world exists another world that is invisible, where all the beings that move in it have a spiritual nature; God rules them all.

God is known as the Father of all spirits and we are spiritual beings who live in a human body. Jesus is the word of God that, voluntarily, accepted to live in a human body. Each word that would come out of his mouth was charged with so much power that even the most skeptic people would say, "No man has ever spoken like this one."

THE BIBLE WAS INSPIRED BY GOD

"All Scripture is given by inspiration of God, and is profitable for doctrine, for reproof, for correction, for instruction in righteousness, that the man of God may be complete, thoroughly equipped for every good work," (2 Timothy 3:16-17).

From the book of Genesis to the book of Revelation, it is all the Word of God. It was written within a period of 1,600 years. The sacred writers who participated were approximately some 40 men; the came from different ages, cultures and social classes.
There were powerful monarchs, famous statesmen, virtuous women, judges, rulers, prophets; aside from, farm workers and fishermen.

God took these men's lives that, for when they met Him, they decided to surrender themselves completely to Him and became channels to bring forth the Word of God, and it stayed recorded thru them and is reserved for each one of us.

It was inspired by God.
The apostle Peter, "For prophecy never came by the will of man, but holy men of God spoke as they were moved by the Holy Spirit," (II Peter 1:21).

It was written and preserved until the end.
The Lord told Isaiah, "Now go, write it before them on a tablet, and note it on a scroll, that it may be for the time to come, forever and ever," (Isaiah 30:8). It was commanded of Daniel, "But you, Daniel, shut up the words, and seal the book until the time of the end; many shall run to and fro, and knowledge shall increase," (Daniel 12:4).

It helps us to know and believe in Jesus.
John said, "And truly Jesus did many other signs in the presence of His disciples, which are not written in this book; but these are written that you may believe that Jesus is the Christ, the Son of God, and that believing you may have life in His name," (John 20:30-31). "So then faith comes by hearing, and hearing by the word of God," (Romans 10:17).

IT IS THE MOST IMPORTANT BOOK

The Bible was the first book printed by Gutenberg; it is the text that has been translated into most languages; it is the most important of all. We never get tired of reading it and we always find new teachings, instructions and revelations in it. Its richness is so abundant that we will never finish understanding it in its entirety. In the Holy Scriptures we find the answers to all the problems in life.

The Word teaches us the guidelines for conquering miracles, it instructs us on the path that leads us to the mount of salvation, it's the map that will lead us to success.

Jesus is the main character.

The main character in the Bible is the Lord Jesus Christ. In times past, each aspect of his ministry, death and resurrection had already been prophesied. Scripture also reveals the facts that will take place in relation to His second coming to this world.

It is our hope.

The Bible is the only book that can takes us from darkness to light, it takes us from death to life, it rescues us from the power of Satan and transfers us to the power of Jesus. It frees us from oppression so that we can be flooded by a glorious peace and it rebukes sickness so we can enjoy full health.

It is the only book that can bring wisdom to our life, hope for our family and a wide scope of eternal glory.

If you read the Bible for only five minutes a day, you will have read its entirety in less than one year. In only 70 hours and 40 minutes we can read the whole Bible; the Old Testament, in 52 hours and 20 minutes, and the New Testament in 18 hours and 20 minutes.

If you read ten chapters a day, four chapters in the morning, two at noon and four at night, you will have finished reading the Bible in only 18 weeks; the Old Testament in 14 weeks and the New Testament in 26 days.

ASPECTS OF THE WORD OF GOD

"Because the Word of God is living and powerful and sharper than any two-edged sword, piercing even to the division of souls and spirit, and of joints and marrow, and is a discerner of the thoughts and intents of the heart," (Hebrews 4:12).

We can see that the Word of God is:

Alive.

The Word of God has so much life that the Lord himself said, "Heaven and earth will pass away, but My words will by no means pass away," (Matthew 24:35). To his disciples, who were not able to comprehend the depth of his words, Jesus said, "It is the Spirit who gives life; the flesh profits nothing. The words that I speak to you are spirit, and they are life," (John 6:63).

Powerful.

From the Greek "energues", which is "operative or dynamite". This means that the Word is charged with all the divine energy and it fulfills the purpose for which God has sent it. "So shall My word be that goes forth from My mouth; it shall not return to Me void, but it shall accomplish what I please, and it shall prosper in the thing for which I sent it," (Isaiah 55:11).

Sharp or emphatic.

More than a two-edged sword (from the Greek "makhaira"). It is like the surgeon's scalpel and it's designed to heal the friend. When the Word of God is loosened, it reaches the most intimate part of your being, healing the deepest wounds of the soul or of the spirit. Being two-edged, (from the Greek "distomos", which literally means "of two mouths"), it penetrates much deeper in the human being, even reaching the joints and the marrow, discerning the thoughts and the intentions of the heart.

When we confess the Word of God with faith, we are loosening spirit of life. Paul said, "Let the Word of Christ dwell in you richly in all wisdom, teaching and admonishing one another in psalms and hymns and spiritual songs, singing with grace in your hearts to the Lord," (Colossians 3:16).

THE WORD OF GOD IS OUR SPIRITUAL FOOD

A. The Milk

"Therefore, rid yourselves of all malice and all deceit, hypocrisy, envy, and slander of every kind. Like newborn babies, crave pure spiritual milk, so that by it you may grow up in your salvation," (I Peter 2:1-2).

What the mother's milk is for the baby, the Word of God is for the newborn Christian. When there is something wrong with the milk, it decomposes and starts to get bitter. If you allow wrong things in your life, the milk of the Word can get bitter, losing therefore its nutritional value. The wrong things can be malice, deceit, hypocrisy, envy and slander. Paul told the Ephesians, "Get rid of all bitterness, rage and anger, brawling and slander, along with every form of malice," (Ephesians 4:31).

The apostle teaches that each one, through his own free will, must get rid of all things that hinder a normal spiritual development and he presents a list of the things that we should never allow or permit in our lives:
- Bitterness
- Rage
- Anger
- Brawling
- Slander
- Malice

It is important to understand that by our own will, we are the we need to get rid of all these things. When we do so, the milk becomes a very nutritive food for our lives.

B. The Bread

Jesus said, "Man does not live by bread alone, but by every word that comes from the mouth of God," (Matthew 4:4).

There comes a time in our Christian life when we learn to depend on God for all our needs; every day we see God's provision just like the Israelites saw it in the desert.

C. The solid food

"For though by this time ye ought to be teachers, you need someone to teach you again the first principles of the oracles of God; and you have come to need milk, and not solid food. For everyone who partakes only of milk is unskillful in the word of righteousness: for he is a babe. But solid food belongs to those who are of full of age, that is, those who by reason of use have their senses exercised to discern both good and evil," (Hebrews 5:12-14).

Solid food is for those who have reached maturity through exercise. Likewise, when an athlete desires to win a championship he must completed be dedicated to the sport; continual practice is what makes him a professional and or a champion.

CONCLUSION

A believer can reach spiritual maturity if he exercises in the study of the Word. The more he studies and goes deep in Scripture, the stronger his senses will be for a normal development.

APPLICATION

Design, along with your students, a list of Bible lessons in chronological order so it can be read in the least time possible according to their level of maturity.

Questionnaire for further study

1. What does the Bible mean for your life?

_____

_____

_____

2. According to what you learned in class concerning the Bible write:

 • It's inspired by God

_____

_____.

 • It was written and preserved until the end

_____

_____.

 • It helps know and believe in Jesus

_____

_____.

3. Why is the Bible the most important book?

_____

_____

_____.

4. Read Hebrews 4:12 and list the characteristics of the word of God:_____

_____

_____.

5. Compare the word of God as your spiritual nourishment:

MILK:_____

_____.

BREAD:_____

_____.

SOLID FOOD _____

_____.

6. Schedule your time and the number of chapters of the Bible that you will read as of today:

DAILY TIME:_____.

NUMBER OF CHAPTERS:_____.

Mark 16:16

The importance
of Baptism

Matthew 3:16-17
Galatians 3:27
Romans 6:3,5
1 Corinthians 12:13
Acts 8:12 and 36-38
Acts 10:47-48
Acts 16:31-34
Luke 3:12

5

LESSON

WHO BELIEVES AND IS BAPTIZED WILL BE SAVED
(Mark 16:16)

God is a God of covenants, and this is the way in which He relates to his people. In the old days he established with Israel the covenant of the circumcision. With the coming of Jesus to this world, he had water baptism established as one of the ways in which we seal our faith and our commitment to Him.

JESUS GAVE US HIS EXAMPLE

Before starting his ministry, the Lord Jesus Christ got close to the Jordan River so that John would baptize him. Because of John's surprise to this act of humility Jesus said, Permit it to be so now, for thus it is fitting for us to fulfill all righteousness." With this statement, the Lord set a precedent: that water baptism is a fundamental requirement of the righteousness of God.

After Jesus was baptized, three things occurred:

- The heavens opened up.
- The Holy Spirit came down on Him like a dove.
- There was a voice from heaven that said, "This is my beloved Son in whom I am well pleased" (Matthew 3:16-17).

In this teaching we see three blessings that cover those who take the step of baptism:

1. The heavens will be open for them.

This means that the relation of man with God, which had been interrupted because of Adam's sin, was restored in Jesus Christ. Now, God moves the heavens so as to tend to his children's need.

2. They will enjoy of a spiritual putting on.

Just like Jesus received the fullness of the Holy Spirit after his baptism, so when the believer steps out in obedience, he puts on the power of God. "For as many of you as have been baptized into Christ have put on Christ" (Galatians 3:27).

3. They will be adopted.

We can hear a voice inside telling us, "You are my beloved son and I am pleased with you." This statement brings tremendous security to our lives because we can feel that we are truly loved by the Father.

Paul said, "For if we have been united together in the likeness of His death (through baptism), certainly we also shall be in the likeness of His resurrection," (Romans 6:5).

"Or do you not know that as many of us as were baptized into Christ Jesus were baptized into His death?" (Romans 6:3)

Baptism symbolizes being buried

The Lord no longer asks us to go to the burial of the cross, for in it He carried our guilt, sin and curse; the only thing He asked was for us to go down to the waters of baptism, which is equivalent to dying on the cross, leaving our whole nature completely crucified there.

Before the Lord went up to heaven, he told his disciples, "Go therefore and make disciples of all the nations, baptizing them in the name of the Father and of the Son and of the Holy Spirit, teaching them to observe all things that I have commanded you; and lo, I am with you always, even to the end of the age," (Matthew 28:19).

The Lord's demands of his disciples were:

- Make disciples of all the nations.
- Baptize them in the name of the Father, of the Son and of the Holy Spirit.
- Teach them to observe all the things that Jesus had commanded them.
- Transmit the assurance the He is with us all the days even to the end of the age.

"For by one Spirit we were all baptized into one body..." (1 Corinthians 12:13).

BAPTISM TAKES PLACE AFTER REPENTANCE

After hearing Peter's anointed message on the Day of Pentecost, the Jews that heard him were moved. They came to the apostles and asked them, "Men and brethren, what shall we do?" Peter answered them saying, "Repent and let everyone of you be baptized in the name of Jesus Christ for the remission of sins; and you shall receive the gift of the Holy Spirit," (Acts 2:38).

The apostle's invitation was:

Repentance.
They knew very well what Peter was trying to say. They were to turn their hearts to God leaving their evil ways behind and purposing to walk down the right path.

Each one's baptism.
Baptism is a personal decision, since it is a covenant. All believers should enter this burial covenant understanding that, although we deserved to die, Jesus did not ask for our death but rather baptism replaces our burial.

Willingness to receive the fullness of the Holy Spirit.
We know that the most important person in the whole universe is the Holy Spirit and God granted Him to us the believers as a gift so we can guard it as a precious pearl.

BAPTISM SHOULD BE AN IMMEDIATE DECISION FOLLOWING CONVERSION

"But when they believed Phillip as he preached the things concerning the kingdom of God and the name of Jesus Christ, both men and women were baptized," (Acts 8:12).

Phillip was the one who shared the Word with an Ethiopian official of Candace, queen of the Ethiopians. This man received the conviction that Scripture is the Word of God and that Jesus is the true Messiah. Going on the way they came to some water, and the eunuch said to Phillip, "See, here is water. What hinders me from being baptized?" Phillip said to him, "If you believe with all your heart, you may." And he answered saying, I believe that Jesus Christ is the Son of God." And he ordered the chariot to stop; and they both went down to the water, Phillip and the eunuch, and he baptized him. (Acts 8:36-38)

After Phillip makes the Scriptures clear to him and he understands that Jesus Christ is the Lord, the eunuch decided to be part of that blessing and he ordered the chariot to stop so he could get baptized.
The only requirement that Phillip demanded was that he has faith: "If you believe with all your heart, you may."

The apostle Peter was preaching the gospel of Jesus in Cornelius' house and, while he was speaking, the Spirit of God descended with power upon all those that heard the message.

They were full of the Holy Spirit.
The same faithful ones of the circumcision that were with Peter were amazed. "Then Peter answered, Can anyone forbid water, that these should not be baptized who have received the Holy Spirit just as we have? And he commanded them to be baptized in the name of the Lord. Then they asked him to stay a few days." (Acts 10:47-48).

Peter's experience with that Gentile family was:

That God approved of them.
The apostle makes this analysis: If God has incorporated them into his people and has made them equal to us, who can get in the way of what God has approved?

He acted quickly.
He didn't wait to receive the opinion of the other Jews, but rather he acted in faith. He took away the barrier of separation that existed between the Jews and the Gentiles thru baptism.

He strengthened them.
He stayed a few days with them in order to instruct them in the Christian faith.

When the apostle Paul preached in the city of Philippi and was imprisoned, the prison doors opened so when the jail keeper saw this, he thought that all the prisoners had fled and was about to kill himself. Paul said to him, "Do yourself no harm, for we are all here." The man trembling, said, "Sirs, what must I do to be saved?" The apostle answered him saying, "Believe on the Lord Jesus Christ and you will be saved, you and your household."
He spoke the Word of God to him, and to all those in his house. And taking them the same hour of the night he washed their wounds, and immediately he and all his family were baptized.
He brought them to his house, set food before them and he rejoiced for having believed in God with all his household," (Acts 16:31-34).

Paul presents the following truths:

- Salvation is extended to the whole house.
- They preached the word to the whole family.
- They baptized the whole family.
- They put their house to Paul's service.

WHOEVER GETS BAPTIZED MUST SHOW FRUITS OF REPENTANCE

When the multitudes would go to John the Baptist to be baptized, he would tell them, after exhorting them strongly, "Therefore bear fruits worthy of repentance," (Luke 3:8).
The fruit is determined by our actions and our words.

When the people would ask him, "What shall we do then?", he answered them saying:

1. Be generous. "He who has two tunics, let him give to him who has none; and he who has food, let him do likewise," (Luke 3:11)

2. Be upright. Then some tax collectors also came to be baptized, and said to him, "What shall we do?" And he said to them, "Collect no more than what is appointed for you."

3. Do not complain about anything. Likewise the soldiers asked him, saying, "And what shall we do?" So he said to them, "Do not intimidate anyone or accuse falsely, and be content with your wages."

CONCLUSION

If Jesus Christ himself, not having sinned, fulfilled the requirement of baptism, how much more we, who need to start a new stage in life, need our old nature and becoming born to the blessing that God has for those who do what His Word says.

APPLICATION

Together with the group, establish a date to baptize all the students.

5 Questionnaire for further study

1. Read, copy and explain the bible text Mark 16:16:

_____

_____

_____ .

2. What happened when Jesus was baptized and what happens today when a person is baptized.

_____

_____

_____ .

3. Answer:

Baptism is a divine commandment because:

_____

_____ .

Baptism is a step of faith that is done after:

_____

_____ .

4. When should we be baptized?

_____

_____ .

5. The blessing of baptism is for those who
(Read Acts 16:31-34) _____

_____ .

6. If you have not been baptized, find out when is the next baptism and register for it!

1 Peter 4:11

CORRESPONDING
BIBLICAL
FOUNDATION

We were created to Bless

Revelation 16:13-14

Psalm 149:6-9

Genesis 1:28

1 Peter 1:7

Genesis 12:1-3

James 3:10

1 Chronicles 17:23

Deuteronomy 28:1-3

1 Corinthians 7:4

Proverbs 10:6a

John 17:9

Job 1:5

Romans 10:8

Proverbs 6:2

John 17:15-17

LESSON

THE TRUE BELIEVER ALWAYS BLESSES

There should always be a word of blessing in your mouth, for there is great power in each word we speak. Peter said, "If anyone speaks, let him speak the oracles of God," (I Peter 4:11). Speaking the words of God puts the spiritual world to work. If they are words of faith and blessing, the whole angelical kingdom starts to operate directed by the Lord. But when negative words are spoken, of bitterness and cursing, the kingdom of darkness comes into play.

"And I saw three unclean spirits like frogs coming out of the mouth of the dragon, out of the mouth of the beast, out of the mouth of the false prophet. For they are spirits of demons, performing signs, which go out to the kings of the earth and of the whole world, to gather them to the battle of the great day of God almighty," (Revelation 16:13-14).

John, as a witness to the heavenly vision, saw the satanic trinity, which is composed of: the dragon, the beast and the false prophet. And from the mouth of each one of them he sees unclean spirits that look like frogs coming out. Something peculiar about these animals is their permanent croaking, especially at night and they don't get tired. This represents people who live complaining, cursing or accusing and don't get tired. It is as if their tongues were controlled by impure spirits. That is why we should be very careful about what comes out of our mouths.

One of the most powerful strategies, demons have to spread filth, is through advertisement and pornography; which have already touched almost all areas of society. Even great businessmen have fallen like victims in the trap, allowing their products to be promoted by women half naked or naked, thinking that's the only way to have success in their business. Most of the advertisement is saturated by a demonic touch through that permanent croaking like frogs.

If your home is going through some crisis, start looking with your eyes of faith at that transformation. And once you have that conviction in your heart, confess with your own words that you already have the best home in the world. Of course, Satan will try to make you tremble, bombarding you with thoughts of doubt and fear; but if you overcome them, you will experience your victory.

Through faith you put to work the angelic armies, and they will help you in the transformation of hearts. You yourself will see the glory of God in your life, in your home, in your ministry and in your business.

EXALTING GOD

"Let the high praises of God be in their mouth, and the two-edged sword in their hand, to execute vengeance on the nations, and punishments on the people; to bind their kings with chains, and their nobles with fetters of iron; to execute on them the written judgment - this honor have all his saints. Praise the Lord!" (Psalm 149:6-9)

When we exalt God with our voice, the Word of God becomes sharper and more powerful in our hands. We have the authority of calling upon the presence of God to take control of the nations, knowing that the people who have opposed the gospel will be broken by the power of His Spirit.

The demonic forces that have controlled individuals, families, cities and nations shall be bound with fetters of iron. Even the demonic powers that were able to get comfortable with no problem, as if they were the kings of the earth, they too shall be bound with chains of iron.

And we will be able to testify to the powers of evil that Jesus Christ has already judged them on the cross of Calvary.

A. The Power of Blessing

When God created man he thought about the blessing. "Then God blessed them, and God said to them, 'Be fruitful and multiply; fill the earth and subdue it; have dominion over the fish of the sea, over the birds of the air, and over every living thing that moves in the earth," (Genesis 1:28).

As we can see, the blessing didn't come to Adam when his was single but when he was married. We must understand that the fullness of the blessings was reserved by God so that the marriage could conquer it.

Three fundamental steps were established by God for the couple:

> Be fruitful
> The word "fruitful" means "life of holiness". The apostle Paul, when he wrote to the Romans, said, "But now, having been set free from sin, and having becomes slaves of God, you have your fruit to holiness, and the end, everlasting life," (Romans 6:22).
> We will only be able to be fruitful when we have been able to break free from the ties of sin. If you want to see God's blessing in all the areas of your life, you should build a life of holiness.
> Saint Peter wrote, "And if you call on the Father, who without partiality judges according to each one's work, conduct yourselves throughout the time of your stay here in fear," (I peter 1:17).
> If you call upon the name of the Holy God, you have to live according to that God whom you are calling upon.

Multiply

Holiness should lead us to multiply. It is God's purpose for us to grow and multiply spiritually, financially or in the ministry.

Have dominion

Holiness leads us to multiply and this guides us to authority. God wants us, as his children, to climb to positions of privilege. His desire is that wherever we are that we have authority and also have an alternative for change; for his purpose is that we be head and not tail.

It is important for those in a marriage, to say the following prayer daily: "God, we present ourselves to you today to receive all your blessings. Thank you for joining us in marriage and for making us participants of the same blessings you gave the first couple, Adam and Eve. We commit ourselves to live in holiness. Give us your grace and your anointing for multiplying our ministerial growth, our spiritual life and our finances. Give us the anointing of authority to be able to guide your work correctly. We ask you in the name of Jesus. Amen.

B. God wants to bless us

"Now the Lord had said to Abram, 'Get out of your country, from your family and from your father's house, to a land that I will show you. I will make you a great nation; I will bless you and make your name great; and you shall be a blessing. I will bless those who bless you, and I will curse him who curses you; and in you all the families of the earth shall be blessed," (Genesis 1:1-3).

In order for God to fulfill his plan of blessing his children, he always seeks to have as a point of contact, the faith of one man and for this one man to become an example for his descendants.

The Hebrew word the jews would use for "blessing" was "beraka", which was equivalent to "transmission or giving of the power of the goodness and favor of God."
Normally, it was transmitted through the spoken word, and for them in the spoken word was the power to attract good or to activate evil.
Each blessing spoken to someone would obey a desire of wanting the favor of God upon that person. James said, "Out of the same mouth proceed blessing and cursing. My brethren, these things ought not to be so," (James 3:10).

We are responsible for the use of words that we speak. We can use them as weapons to destroy or as tools to edify. If you have chosen the way of blessing, you should purpose in your heart to daily bless those that are around you.

THE POWER OF BLESSING
GIVEN BY GOD

"And now, O Lord, the word which You have spoken concerning Your servant and concerning his house, let it be established forever, and do as You have said," (1 Chronicles 17:23).

Here David takes a hold of a promise of blessing given by God for his life, and claimed the fulfillment of the same. God cannot change what has come out of his lips. His Word remains firm in the heavens for He fulfills everything he has promised his children.

"Now it shall come to pass, if you diligently obey the voice of the Lord your God, to observe carefully all His commandments which I command you today, that the Lord your God will set you high above all nations of the earth. And all these blessings shall come upon you and overtake you, because you obey the voice of the Lord your God. Blessed shall you be in the city, and blessed shall you be in the country," (Deuteronomy 28:1-3).

This passage teaches us that the blessings that God desires to give us were subject to our obedience to his Word. Once this requirement is fulfilled, we are partakers of the blessings given to his people Israel. "And all these blessings shall come upon you and overtake you," (vs. 3).

The following verses specify the types of blessings that we can be beneficiaries to because of our obedience: family, financial, emotional, business, territorial and spiritual.

> Prayer: God, I have made a covenant of living according to your Word and I claim blessing upon my life and the lives of my beloved ones. I ask for a blessing upon my health and the health of my family. I ask for a financial provision and that everything I touch have your blessing. Prosper us in such a way that we may be able to bless others through our finances. Give us creative ideas and the strength to make riches. Father, I ask you in the name of Jesus.

The husband blesses the wife.

Paul said the husband has authority over his wife's body (1 Corinthians 7:4). If God has given us this tremendous responsibility over the life of our wife, let's give it the appropriate use. And the best way to do it is by blessing her.

> Blessing: My wife, I give thanks to God for your life and because He chose you to be my companion. May God make you grow in stature as He did with Ruth and Esther; may you find favor in the eyes of God and those that surround you; may the Lord bless the work of your hands and everything you do. I know that the promises of Proverbs 31 are a reality in your life. You have been an excellent wife, an example of a mother and a leader, which everyone admires. May the Lord bless you with health, with peace, and make you a thousand times more than what you already are. In the name of Jesus, Amen.

The father blesses his children.
"Blessings are on the head of the righteous," (Proverbs 10:6a). I pray for them. I do not pray for the world but for those whom You have given Me, for they are Yours" (Juan 17:9).

God had given us a family and it is our job to bless each one of them. Job was in the habit of sanctifying each one of his sons daily (Job 1:5).
The blessing that you loosen upon your children is the prophetic word you impart on their lives. Paul said, "The word is near you, in your mouth and in your heart; that is, the word of faith which we preach," (Romans 10:8).

The word you loosen upon your children you must first believe it in your heart. This should not be done as something formal, just to fulfill a requirement, for we know we are bound to the words that we speak (Proverbs 6:2).

In the same manner that Isaac asked his son to come close in order to bless him, the father should bring his children close and speak blessing upon each one of them; and should pray individually for their lives.

Blessing upon the daughters:

> Daughter, I give thanks to God for your life. You are a gift from God for our home. May the Lord make you like Ruth or Esther; may you find favor in the eyes of God and of men; may the Lord keep your emotions from any hurt; may the Father give you for a husband a man fearful of God, that loves you, takes care of you and protects you. That you be an excellent wife, a good mother and a great leader. May the Lord make you prosper and over abound in goods and wisdom. May He give you the desires of your heart and make you a thousand times more than what you are now. In the name of Jesus, Amen.

Blessing upon the sons:

Son, I give thanks to God for your life. I bless you with the blessing of Abraham, Isaac and Jacob. May the Lord's hand be upon you and make you His servant. May the Lord bless you with wisdom, with prosperity and with peace. That every day you live you use it to enlarge His kingdom. May the Lord give you for a wife a virtuous woman, and that you be an example for her. May God make you a thousand times more than what you are now. In the name of Jesus, Amen.

Blessing the disciples.
"Speak to Aaron and his sons, saying, this is the way you shall bless the children of Israel, say to them: The Lord bless you and keep you; the Lord make his face shine upon you, and be gracious to you; the Lord lift up his countenance upon you, and give you peace," (Numbers 6:23-26).

Our disciples come to be as sons and we should pray for them daily and bless them, for many of them are the ones carrying the burden of the ministry and they need our permanent cover of prayer.
Jesus prayed for his disciples that they always be protected by God: "I do not pray that you should take them out of the world, but that you should keep them from the evil one. They are not of the world, just as I am not of the world. Sanctify them by your truth. Your word is truth" (John 17:15-17).

Prayer: Father, I give you thanks for each of my disciples. I bless them today with the blessing of Abraham, Isaac and Jacob. I ask that the power of God keep them away from all evil and danger, that they may understand the purpose of your call and fulfill it faithfully, and make them a thousand times more than what they are now. In the name of Jesus, Amen.

CONCLUSION

The purpose of God since the beginning of humanity has been to bless his children with fruit, multiplication and authority. The decision of accepting the challenge and the responsibility of being that channel of blessing for their loved ones in the spiritual area, emotional, physical, financial and ministerial is in their hands.

APPLICATION

Each student will learn the value of loosening words of blessing upon their life, their home, their ministry and their job. It is very important to sanctify the fountain of life, which are the words and impart life and power to every adverse situation by our words.

6 Questionnaire for further study

1. What is the meaning of the word Bless:

_____

_____

_____.

2. According to Genesis 1:28, explain the power of the blessing given by the Lord:

BE FRUITFUL _____

_____

_____.

MULTIPLY_____

_____

_____.

HAVE DOMINION_____

_____

_____.

3. Activate the power of the blessing through a prayer for your:

SPOUSE:_____

_____

_____

_____

_____.

CHILDREN:_____

_____

_____

_____

_____.

BIBLICAL
FOUNDATIONAL
REFERENCE

Ephesians 3:14-15

CORRESPONDING
BIBLICAL
FOUNDATION

The blessing of
Fatherhood

Matthew 13:3-8
Matthew 5:48
Deuteronomy 18:21
Hosea 4:6

7

LESSON

THE BLESSING OF
BEING A FATHER

"For this reason I bow my knees to the Father of our Lord Jesus Christ, from whom the whole family in heaven and earth is named," (Ephesians 3:14-15).

Never before in the history of humanity has the world asked with so much insistence that fathers take on their responsibility and to take the place of fatherhood that belongs to them. Our present society moves forward at such a rapid pace that more and more of it demands time from people. In order to fulfill these demands, sacrifice the time that belongs to their children.

How well the parable of the sower applies to the lives of many fathers. "Behold, a sower went out to sow. And as he sowed, some seed fell by the wayside, and the birds came and devoured them. Some fell on stony places, where they did not have much earth; and they immediately sprang up because they had no depth of earth. But when the sun was up they were scorched, and because they had no root they withered away. And some fell among thorns, and the thorns sprang up and choked them. But others fell on good ground and yielded a crop: some as hundredfold, some sixty, some thirty," (Matthew 13:3-8).

Each time a child asks his father for some time to share with him, a type of mental bombardment occurs in the man's mind bringing different pretexts so as not to make a commitment to his son. Some don't do it with evil intentions. They think they'll have the necessary time later on to do so.

That is the adversary's strategy to rob one of the most important treasures children can have: their memories.

On the way. Matthew 13:4
We find Satan robbing from the minds of the fathers their desire to share time with their children.

On stony places. Matthew 13:5
It is when fathers get excited and promise to spend time with them but a few days later, all the emotion disappears. They forget about what was promised, and the children were left with the frustration of not having been able to share their moments with their parents.

Among thorns. Matthew 13:7
It is when fathers are waiting to take some time to dedicate to their children, but every day that goes by they get more and more entangled in other commitments.

On good ground. Matthew 13:8
It is when the father has equilibrium, he knows how to administer his time and he gives the best part to his family. This is what children truly remember with much warmth.

Fathers must understand that children need to strengthen every area of their life and if teamwork is accomplished, this would be of great help and of blessing.

THE CHILDREN'S IDENTITY

Every person desires to know who he is and where is he going. We are living in very difficult times. Parents mistreat their children based on the concept that they are educating them. But let me show you that discipline is never for hurting, but rather to shape.

One of the greatest crises in the life of children comes about due to abandonment.

I spoke with a woman who had three children. She had already had three marriages and she felt the present one was on very rocky ground. That woman opened her heart to me and told me, "I never met my dad. He abandoned us when I was a little girl. I always had an emotional emptiness caused by the lack of having a father.

A certain day, I was so desperate to know who my father was that I took the telephone book and called every person that had the same name and last name as his. I wanted to at least talk with him, even if just for a moment. But it was all in vain." With tears in her eyes she told me, "I need to know where I come from, who I am and where am I going."

If parents could understand the harm they cause their children, they would try to have more dominion over their impulses and they would make more of an effort to raise a family more sure of itself. Due to that emotional emptiness produced by the lack of a father, that woman had gone through many sentimental failures.

Together with my wife we have purposed to do everything possible so as not to leave any wounds in the emotions of our daughters. We try for them to have nice memories of their parents, but we know this is accomplished through example, for no one can fake it in front of their children. A man cannot fake being in love with his wife.

When there is true love, it is shown in how he treats her, it is transmitted through respect, it is shown in how he honors her, you can see it in how he gives her all his support.

If a man is a good husband, he will also be a good father, for what children most admire is a good marriage relationship.

When we truly find out who we are, we understand the blessing of having a father because it gives us the security in knowing there is someone interested and worried about us. I have four daughters and I know my opinion is very important to them. In everything they do, they are always wanting to know their dad's stance.

When Sara, the youngest, has an achievement, whether it be in sports or in any other area, she tells me, "Daddy, isn't it true I'm the best?" And I answer her, "Of course, daughter, you always beat the others." I know that for children the voice of encouragement and motivation that parents give, is fundamental.

PROVIDE SECURITY FOR
THEIR CHILDREN

There is great security in the family environment when the father is the head of the home because generally, the protector of the home is more the man than the woman.

Many years ago we were climbing a mountain with one of my daughters who was only four years old. When we had gone a short way she got tired and the only thing she could do was raise her arms so I could pick her up. She didn't care if her dad was also tired, she simply raised her arms because she knew there was security and rest in her father's arms. We constantly find in Scripture God revealing Himself as a loving Father who provides security for his children. God is the father of excellence, and from him all fatherhood in heaven takes His name. The Lord Jesus marked one of the highest goals any man can reach: to be a true father. "Therefore you shall be perfect, just as your Father in heaven is perfect," (Matthew 5:48).

One of the problems society has had to confront nowadays is seeing how more and more technology has put a distance between the members of the family.

The virtual friends have replaced the communication and relationship of the family.

For that reason, it is imperative that both parents and children make an effort to establish the means of getting closer, leaving aside all the obstacles that have hindered their joy of a good communication.

For this to happen it is necessary to:

- Daily set out a time. Children don't ask for a lot, just take them into consideration. If you start with fifteen minutes, his will be a great start.

- Talk with them. Avoid raising your voice, reproaching, using satires, complaining or rubbing in mistakes. Let everything you share while you talk be positive, be of faith and motivation for them.

- Create an environment favorable for communication. When there have been offenses and forgiveness has not been asked, the environment can become very tense. It is very important to correct the wounds from the past and get rid of all resentment.

- Have recreational activities. And this way, integrate each one of the children according to their ages.

- Consider or include them when important family decision is being made.

- Treat them as you treat your friends. Pay attention to them when they speak to you, when they share their achievements and victories, as well as when they unload their frustrations.

Make them feel they are the most important people for you. Verbalize it and express it with terms of endearment.

AS A FAMILY TRY TO MAINTAIN CONTACT WITH THE WORD

"Therefore you shall lay up these words of mine in your heart and in your soul, and bind them as a sign on your hand, and they shall be frontlets between your eyes. You shall teach them to your children, speaking of them when you sit in your house, when you walk by the way, when you lie down, and when you rise up. And you shall write them on the doorposts of your house and on your gates, that your days and the days of your children may be multiplied in the land of which the Lord swore to your fathers to give them, like the days of the heavens above the earth" (Deuteronomy 11:18-21).

The blessing God has for the family should come down through the parents. It is the father's job to teach the Word of God to each one of his children. He should continually repeat the Word next to his children, until every teaching and principle be a way of life in the home.
In Hosea 4:6 it says, "My people are destroyed for lack of knowledge. Because you have rejected knowledge, I also will reject you from being priest for Me; because you have forgotten the law of your God, I also will forget your children." Parents, listen to this truth. If you forget the Word of God, God will forget your children.
We hear stories of men who did evil, men who affected the nation with violence, men who were cold and insensible, but when their children were touched, they were hurt so deeply that they were broken because that was their weak side.

CONCLUSION

Fathers, don't allow judgment to touch your children. From now on, you can teach them and advise them to turn to God, and live according to His Word. Don't be tolerant with them in regards to evil. Instruct them in the fear of God; establish principles that will help them live according to the Word; give them time, the attention, the care and the respect they require in order for them to live balanced and successful lives.

APPLICATION

Establish a list of specific steps that will favor your relationship with your children and implement them immediately, writing down your achievements and progress. Accept your fatherhood and start exercising it with joy.

7 Questionnaire for further study

1. What is the best memory you have of your father?

_____
_____
_____.

2. What would you like your child remember you for?

_____
_____
_____.

3. If you compare the parable of the sower in relationship with your children where do you think the seed of fatherhood has been planted? Mark with an x:
- In the way_____
- In rocks_____
- In thorns_____
- Good soil_____

4. Through a specific action how can you establish the following in your children:

IDENTITY:_____
_____.

BALANCED SELF-ESTEEM:_____
_____.

SECURITY:_____
_____.

DIALOGUE:_____
_____.

DAILY CONTACT WITH THE WORD:_____
_____.

5. Purpose yourself to have a special time were you share together with each of your children.

BIBLICAL
FOUNDATIONAL
REFERENCE

1 Thessalonians 5:24

CORRESPONDING
BIBLICAL
FOUNDATION

Knowing the
will of God

Genesis 25:23

Romans 8:5-8

Psalm 73:27

Romans 8:9-11

Jeremiah 1:5

Genesis 25:32

Matthew 4:3-4

Job 2:4

Hebrews 12:16-17

Genesis 32:26

2 Corinthians 12:9

Esther 5:2-3

Romans 12:2

2 Corinthians 3:18

2 John 2:17

8

LESSON

Although I had been reading the Bible for a few months, I still didn't know Jesus personally and I continued being a slave to vices and to sin. One particular night a thought came to my mind which later I understood could only come from the Holy Spirit: "What good things has your vice given you?" My answer was, "No vice can leave anything good." Later another thought came: "Try prayer, to see what answer you'll get." This proposal seemed so sensible that I told myself, "I don't think I have anything to lose if I try prayer."

That same night I made the decision to have an appointment with God. The following day I was in the living room of my house opening up my heart for Jesus to take complete control of my life. That night Jesus came into my being; he transformed my heart and filled me with the Holy Spirit.

The will of God came to my life as a seed, through an idea but fell on good ground for, as I accepted it, it produced fruit of salvation. Had I allowed doubt to come in, I would have strayed from his will and been out of his purpose.

Paul said, "He who calls you is faithful, who also will do it," (1 Thessalonians 5:24)

1. THE CARNAL MAN

"Two nations are in your womb, two peoples shall be separated from your body; one people shall be stronger than the other, and the older shall serve the younger" (Genesis 25:23).

Rebecca felt the oppression of two natures struggling within her womb. Both being fought continually and she sought divine guidance when being tired, she wanted to die. But in the struggle, God revealed to her that the firstborn would be the second to come out.

Jacob represents the spiritual man and Esau represents the carnal man.

We should understand that the will of God is with those that are willing to lead a life in the spirit.

"For those who live according to the flesh set their minds on the things of the flesh, but those who live according to the Spirit, the things of the Spirit. For to be carnally minded is death, but to be spiritually minded is life and peace. Because the carnal mind is enmity against God; for it is not subject to the law of God, nor indeed can be. So then, those who are in the flesh cannot please God," (Romans 8:5-8).

The carnal man is he who desires to depend on himself without taking God into consideration and since he knows that God does not approve of what he does, he prefers to live far from Him. The carnal man is characterized because:
- He thinks about carnal things.
- He occupies himself with things that lead to death.
- His plans are enmity against God.
- He is rebellious and is not subject to God's law.

Evildoers are rebels without a cause and their rebellion has taken them to a spiritual death. "For indeed, those who are far from You shall perish; You have destroyed all those who desert You," (Psalm 73:27).

2. THE SPIRITUAL MAN

"But you are not in the flesh but in the Spirit, if indeed the Spirit of God dwells in you. Now, if anyone does not have the Spirit of Christ, he is not His. And if Christ is in you, the body is dead because of sin, but the Spirit is life because of righteousness. But if the Spirit of Him who raised Jesus from the dead dwells in you, He who raised

Christ from the dead will also give life to your mortal bodies through His Spirit who dwells in you," (Romans 8:9-11).

The spiritual man is characterized because:

- He lives according to the Spirit. This refers to a complete rendering to the will of God.
- He lives by the righteousness of faith. This occurs when the spiritual man has overcome the carnal nature.
- The spirit of Christ dwells in him.

God knows us even before our birth and has sent us to this world with a specific mission. "Before I formed you in the womb I knew you, before you were born I set you apart; I appointed you as a prophet to the nations" (Jeremiah 1:5 NIV).

3. FREEDOM TO CHOOSE

"But Jacob said, "Sell me your birthright as of this day." And Esau said, "Look, I am about to die; so what is this birthright to me?" (Genesis 25:32).

Esau's decision of selling his birthright was not as a result of pressure that he felt from God. God greatly respects the freedom to choose which He gave each human being. Man's behavior is determined by the ideas he accepts into his mind. Esau stood before two roads: his physical desire and his birthright, by which he would inherit all the blessings of Abraham and of his father Isaac. God should have been remembered as "the God of Abraham, of Isaac and of Esau," but since he didn't see an immediate response, Esau despised the birthright.

The thought he accepted came directly from the adversary, "What have you gotten by being the firstborn? It's best if you sell it before dying of hunger.

You remember when Jesus was tempted in the wilderness, "...if You are the Son of God, command that these stones become bread. But He answered and said, "It is written, Man shall not live by bread alone, but by every word that proceeds from the mouth of God," (Matthew 4:3-4). The strategy the adversary uses is to drop seeds through thoughts; it's equivalent to putting bait to control your life. Satan applied an old principle that he had also used with Job. "A man will give all he has for his own life," (Job 2:4).

The adversary has used the desires of the flesh to blind the eyes of the spirit and in doing so, blocking the understanding in order to prevent hearing the voice of God. He guides them to act clumsily so later he can have dominion over them.

The writer to the Hebrews warns us, "Lest there be any fornicator or profane person like Esau, who for one morsel of food sold his birthright. For you know that afterward, when he wanted to inherit the blessing, he was rejected, for he found no place for repentance, though he sought it diligently with tears," (Hebrews 12:16-17).

4. HOW TO MOVE THE HAND OF GOD

"And He said, "Let me go, for the day breaks." But he said, "I will not let You go unless You bless me!" (Genesis 32:26).

The most distressed night for Jacob was when he knew his brother Esau was coming for him. The memory of the threats came back to his mind. He started to feel the terror of death was taking over him because he felt the destruction of his house gaining up on him at full gallop. This led him to take refuge in prayer. This was a very decisive hour for Jacob; Either God was going to intervene or evil was going to get him.

The prayer that night was so intense but at the end he felt the deliverance of his soul. It's interesting the name Jacob calls that place: God face (Peniel).

All the pressure that had been brewing in the spiritual realm disappeared; fear was gone, the anguish and despair had left. There came such a peace and confidence in his life as if an army of millions of angels were with him. The next day, when he met up with his brother, Jacob finally had control over the circumstances because he had spent the whole night battling to obtain the blessing, and he had achieved it. "But Esau ran to meet him, and embraced him, and fell on his neck and kissed him, and they wept" (Genesis 33:4).

What happened that caused his brother to change his attitude so abruptly? These are the miracles that prayer produces because prayer changes things. Jacob said, "No, please, if I have now found favor in your sight, then receive my present from my hand, in as much as I have seen your face as though I had seen the face of God, and you were pleased with me," (Genesis 33:10).
In other words, Jacob was telling him, "I am experiencing the same thing I lived last night, where while I was praying, I saw this favor that you are now having towards me today."

5. LEANING ON GOD

"Just as he crossed over Peniel the sun rose on him, and he limped on his hip," (Genesis 32:31).

Jacob had always done what he wanted to do. He always accomplished what he would set out to do, without considering the means he would use to accomplish it. The experience with the angel changed his life in a radical way. One of the things the angel had to do with Jacob was to leave him limping. This implies that, from that day on, Jacob had to use a cane to lean on.

This speaks to us about a life of faith, where it is no longer our strength that counts, but rather the measure of faith we may have. God had to tell Paul, "My grace is sufficient for you, for My strength is made perfect on weakness" (2 Corinthians 12:9).

The sun rose on Jacob.

The sun is a symbol that we have found grace in the eyes of God, in the same way as when King Ahasuerus held out to Queen Esther the golden scepter that was in his hand and said, "What do you wish, Queen Esther? What is your request? It shall be given to you, up to half the kingdom!" (Esther 5:2-3). To find favor in the eyes of God implies that circumstances are transformed by the divine power and we start to live in a period of mercy, in which God and legions of angels are at our disposition and will help us to conquer our victories.

6. RENEWING OUR WALK WITH GOD

"And do not be conformed to this world, but be transformed by the renewing of your mind, that you may prove what is that good and acceptable and perfect will of God" (Romans 12:2).

One of the greatest dilemmas a person lives is having to confront the unknown, for this may produce fear, uncertainty, and doubt. From the moment God created us, he gave us a spirit of conquest. In order to conquer the spiritual realm, we must maintain our mind renewed constantly.
We know that the Swiss were the pioneers in watch making but since they didn't take the innovating risk when they had the opportunity of implementing the digital watch, the Japanese beat them to it in this area.

We must understand that many things that were very useful in the past, perhaps are no longer today.

Renewing our minds keeps us always active, just like the river that runs down the stream maintains its water fresh all the time.

Each day is different from the next.
That is why Paul said, "But we all, with unveiled face, beholding as in a mirror the glory of the Lord, are being transformed into the same image from glory to glory, just as by the spirit of the Lord," (2 Corinthians 3:18).

We must understand that God's will for us:

Is good.
God has prepared the richest blessings for us to enjoy, in the same manner as a loving father who wants to give his children the best.

Is acceptable.
God is very careful and everything He gives his children is usually satisfying. God does not give a man a woman so she'll make his life miserable; nor does He prosper him financially and let him be afflicted with a disease; no. We know that God's blessing enriches and does not add sadness to it.

Is perfect.
The word perfect speaks to us about something that is complete. God never leaves anything undone. He has given us all things so we may enjoy them abundantly. He has not given us his Spirit by measure. He never gives us small blessings but rather all his blessings are immense. David said, "I delight to do Your will, O my God, and Your law is within my heart," (Psalm 40:8). The apostle John said, "And the world is passing away, and the lust of it, but he who does the will of God abides forever," (1 John 2:17).

CONCLUSION

Finding the way to perfection in the Lord will depend on your willingness to hear the sweet voice of the Holy Spirit and to follow his way with no reservations until you see that the will of God in your life is good, acceptable and perfect. Then you will behave as a spiritual being and will be able to start to live in the supernatural dimension.

APPLICATION

Each student is to turn in a written list of at least five attitudes he needs to change, that will allow him to stop being a carnal man and will make him into a spiritual man.

8 Questionnaire for further study

1. Explain the difference between the carnal man and the spiritual man with an example:

_____

_____

_____.

2. Complete:
   a. The carnal man thinks in the _____
   b. Is occupied _____
   c. His intentions are_____
   d. Is rebellious because:_____

3. The spiritual man is characterized by:

_____

_____.

4. Explain why the will of God for your life is:

   GOOD:_____

   _____.

   ACCEPTABLE:_____

   _____.

   PERFECT_____

   _____

   _____.

5. According to Romans 12:2; explain how you can renew your walk with God

_____

_____

_____.

BIBLICAL
FOUNDATIONAL
REFERENCE

1 John 5:4

CORRESPONDING
BIBLICAL
FOUNDATION

1 John 3:9
Philippians 4:6
1 Corinthians 2:11-12
James 4:71
1 Corinthians 2:16
Isaiah 45:7
Numbers 13:30-31
Numbers 14:28
Proverbs 12:14
Ecclesiastes 10:12

Think like a
Conqueror

LESSON

"Because everything that is born of God overcomes the world; and this is the victory that has overcome the world, even our faith," (I John 5:4).

The apostle John presents us with the two basic aspects every conqueror should have:
a) Be born of God.
b) Have faith.

1. BE BORN OF GOD

Jesus taught us how we could be born of God: "Unless one is born of water and the Spirit, he cannot enter the kingdom of God," (John 3:5). Water speaks about baptism, while to be born of the Spirit is the result of having accepted Jesus in your heart as Lord and Savior of your life. This step of faith and obedience produces conception deep within our heart rises within us; this is the same nature of Jesus that has started to grow through faith. "That Christ may dwell in your hearts through faith," (Ephesians 3:17a).

When this conception in our hearts takes place, the spirit world is opens in our lives; and then through the studying of the word, prayer and having fellowship with other believers, we grow and strengthen ourselves in God. John said, "Whoever has been born of God does not sin, for His seed remains in him, and he cannot sin, because he has been born of God," (I John 3:9). Our spiritual nature keeps us from the traps of deceit and of sin.

2. OUR FAITH

Faith is not human, it is not material, is not emotional nor intellectual. Faith can only come from a spiritual nature; and can only grow in those that have rendered their lives to Jesus Christ. Faith makes us partakers of the same nature as Christ. Everything that occurs in the life of faith, pertains to the spiritual nature. Faith cannot be faked, you cannot imitate it, for when trials come, only those that have faith can withstand. We know that without faith it is impossible to please God. The smallest faith can move the largest mountain. Overcomers need only have the faith the size of a mustard seed in order to do great quests.

Faith should be in everything we do. Faith is believing what God said, faith is believing the Word of God. If you want to have faith but ignore this book, you are depositing it within yourself and not in what God says. Faith and fear are in conflict. Genuine faith frees us from fear. Through faith, we go forward and conquer.

3. PROTECTING OUR THOUGHTS

The enemy works through our thoughts because he knows that if people accept his ideas in their mind, he can easily conquer their will. So then, he starts shooting all kinds of darts. If we don't accept them in our mind and our will remains firm, we will suffer no damage. But whoever falls to the devil's trap and accepts them, these thoughts are so strong that they begin working within that person for the purpose of breaking their will. And when this occurs, that person is left spiritually unprotected. They come to be as a city without walls, very easily conquered.

Solomon said, "For as he thinks in his heart, so is he." We are the end result of our thoughts and these are expressed through words.

Your mind is a treasure of richness. Do not allow the enemy to bombard you with destructive and negative thoughts. Even if it were possible to build a computer as big and powerful as the largest building ever, it would not be able to produce not a single thought.

God gave man the capability to create ideas and we should channel these ideas for blessings.

Change your thoughts, don't accept failure. Set monthly, weekly and daily goals. Don't allow any thought of doubt to enter into your mind. Don't speak negatively. If you can achieve your goal of not speaking anything negative for a whole day, extend it for a week. Once you achieve this, extend it for a month. And if you can accomplish it, extend it for a year. This way you are becoming a conqueror. Paul said, "Be anxious for nothing, but in everything by prayer and supplication, with thanksgiving, let your requests be made known to God," (Philippians 4:6).

Emerson said, "What is ahead of us and behind us is insignificant, compared to what is within us." Within us is the potential for life. Thoughts and ideas are fertilized there.

4. MAINTAINING A GOAL OPENED TO INNOVATION

Let's not look for the easiest route. If we want successful things, we have to invest time. For sure we will see the reward for every effort we make to achieve something. I have learned that the innovation of the mind needs to be daily. God has shown me that the day in which we do not change, that will be the day we become legalistic. We should be very open-minded everyday in order to understand what God wants us to do. Innovation prevents man from falling into monotony, for everyday there are new challenges. Calderon de la Barca said, "Who keep thoughts in control which so often are so light and subtle? For these have no body, they go through walls, they go through chests and can see the most hidden parts of the soul."

We must understand that behind every thought there is a spiritual being that promotes them. The thoughts we have allowed into our minds are the ones that determine our personality. Paul said, "For what man knows the things of a man except the spirit of the man which is in him? Even so no one knows the things of God except the Spirit of God. Now we have received, not the spirit of the world, but the Spirit who is from God, that we might know the things that have been freely given to us by God," (I Corinthians 2:11-12). What a great blessing it is to know that our thoughts are directed by God!

5. HAVING THE MIND OF CHRIST

Think on this: What did the Lord Jesus think about?

Everything Jesus thought about was tied to the Word. That is why you'll find Him saying, "To do your will is my desire." Every word Jesus would say already had the heavenly Father's approval. He never allowed his mind to be idle. When Satan came along to try to influence his thoughts, He told him, "Depart from me for it is written: Man shall not live by bread alone." In three occasions he mentioned the words, "It is written," until the adversary left Him. James said, "Therefore submit yourselves to God. Resist the devil and he will flee from you," (James 4:7).

"For who has known the mind of the Lord that he may instruct Him? But we have the mind of Christ," (1 Corinthians 2:16).

"You love righteousness and hate wickedness; therefore God, your God, has anointed you with the oil of gladness more than your companion," (Psalm 45:7). Among the things the prophet could see about Jesus' nature was that Jesus was the happiest man on earth; and that that joy was an anointing given by God. In other words, joy comes as a result of a life of holiness, where love of righteousness has grown and in our hearts we make the decision of getting away from any kind of evil.

A. THOUGHTS OF CONQUEST

"Then Caleb quieted the people before Moses, and said, 'Let us go up at once and take possession, for we are well able to overcome it.' But the men who had gone with him said, 'We are not able to go up against the people, for they are stronger than we,'" (Numbers 13:30-31).

Joshua presents three steps in order to take hold of that which God wants to deliver into their hands:

Let us go up

The life of faith implies an effort on our part and it is completely opposite to the life of sin. Sin always takes people down the easier road which implies a downhill life. Faith demands our effort, which is to go up the mountain where there are difficulties but with the complete certainty that we will overcome them.

Let us take possession

Joshua was completely sure of being superior to the enemies that they had to confront since the power of God had weakened them and They also had already been assured by the Lord that they would have a great victory. This was the opportunity of making a reality of God's promises to his people.

We are more able then they

In other words, the ones with us are more than the ones with them. Joshua was completely convinced in his heart that God had already given them the victory. But the spirit of discouragement had come to prevent the triumph. That is the reason why Joshua puts himself in the gap to try to make the people reconsider to not let escape this great opportunity pass by. Unfortunately, everything was in vain because discouragement had already taken its toll on most of the people.

"But the men who had gone with him said, 'We are not able to go up against the people, for they are stronger than we,'" (Numbers 13:31). The lesson God wanted to give to the people of Israel was that, although they would confront people much greater than they, God would move his angelic armies and they would fall easily, being reduced to nothing. But the enemy had already used the circumstances in the minds of these ten princes of Israel; and because of this, they thought they were going to have to confront these giants with their own strength.

When they took their eyes off God and didn't think about the help they would receive from Him, they got discouraged and became faint. They got away from faith by trying to put logic to the situation. And without faith it is impossible to please God.

"If the Lord delights in us, then He will bring us into this land and give it to us, a land which flows with milk and honey. Only do not rebel against the Lord, nor fear the people of the land, for they are our bread; the protection has departed from them, and the Lord is with us. Do not fear them. And all the congregation said to stone them with stones," (Numbers 14:8-10).

Find favor
- We can only please God when we live a life of faith; and the life of faith is depending totally on God. When we do this, the best blessings will be reserved for us.

Do not be rebellious

- Rebellion is not wanting to conquer things according to how God has planned it. And discouragement came due to the negativism, and this lead the people to rebellion.

Nor fear the people

- To fear the people whom you have to confront means you accept the supremacy they have on your life. We will not be able to conquer that which we fear.

They are our bread

- This expression illustrates how easy victory would be, that without much effort they would defeat them. Joshua already knew God was on his side and that no one could stand in His presence. But the answer the people gave Joshua for having spoken the language of faith was that he should be stoned to death. For an unbelieving people, discouraged and whining, faith is a language that bothers their eyes.

THE POWER OF WORDS OF FAITH

"As I live, says the Lord, just as you have spoken in My hearing, so I will do to you," (Numbers 14:28). Joshua and Caleb were the only ones of the ten spies who spoke in a different way. They decided to believe God, and they tried to have the people move in faith and take possession of the land. God was pleased with them that He told Moses, "But My servant Caleb, because he has a different spirit in him and has followed Me fully, I will bring into the land where he went, and his descendants shall inherit it," (Numbers 14:24).

THE DEVASTATING EFFECTS
OF WORDS OF COMPLAINTS

On the other hand, the majority of the people had complained against God, saying, "If only we had died in this wilderness! Why has the Lord brought us to this land to fall by the sword, that our wives and children should become victims? Would it not be better for us to return to Egypt?" (Numbers 14:2-3). God's answer to the people was, Each word you have expressed, has become a creed. And that is exactly what I'll do; you will die in the desert. Your children shall bear the brunt of your rebellion until you are consumed in the desert.

"Those very men who brought the evil report about the land, died by the plague before the Lord. But Joshua the son of Nun and Caleb the son of Jephunneh remained alive, of the men who went to spy out the land," (Numbers 14:37-38).

B. HAVE A THANKFUL HEART

The door to reach the presence of God is called "thanksgiving". No one can enjoy God's presence until thanksgiving rests in their heart. By confessing God's promises before the people, Joshua and Caleb were honoring Him before the whole congregation. And after forty years, they were the leaders that brought the people of Israel into the promised land.

THE WISE MAN'S WORDS
AND THE FOOL'S WORDS

Solomon said, "A man will be satisfied with good by the fruit of his mouth, and the recompense of a man's hands will be rendered to him," (Proverbs 12:14).

"The words of a wise man's mouth are gracious, but the lips of a fool shall swallow him up," (Ecclesiastes 10:12).

"A fool's mouth is his destruction, and his lips are the snare of his soul," (Proverbios 18:7).

CONCLUSION

The results our heart yearns to have will depend largely on our attitudes and thoughts. Let's make an effort to obtain and retain the mind of Christ, to have a renewed mind of conquest, and a willingness to have God's will established in our own life, in our family, work and group of twelve.

APPLICATION

The mind of a conqueror in the life of any believer should mean the beginning of a life of success, of conquest and possess the promises that our God has given us in the different areas of our lives; in our relationship with God, with all people, our family, our ministry, our finances, our work and our health.

9 Questionnaire for further study

1. Read and explain: I John 5:4

_____

_____

_____.

2. What does "Born of God" imply?

_____

_____

_____.

3. Why and how should I protect my thoughts? _____

_____

_____

_____.

4. Reflect and Analyze:

    a. What thoughts did Jesus have? _____

    _____

    _____.

    b. Are your thoughts like Jesus' thoughts?

    _____

    _____.

5. Through a prayer, give thanks to God for the thoughts He has of you and ask Him for words of wisdom for your lips.

_____

_____.

BIBLICAL
FOUNDATIONAL
REFERENCE

Proverbs 3:9-10

CORRESPONDING
BIBLICAL
FOUNDATION

God created man so he would be Prosperous

1 Timothy 6:17
Hebrews 11:4
Mark 12:30
John 3:16
Genesis 22:16-17
Proverbs 10:7
1 Chronicles 29:12
2 Corinthians 9:7-9
Proverbs 11:25
Hebrews 7:2-6
Genesis 28:20-22
Malachi 3:10-12

LESSON

It took the Lord five days of creation in order to be able to prepare with a wealth of detail everything man needed to know so he would have no need of anything. God was so generous with man that in creation itself, He prepared the provision for generations to come, so that there would be enough natural resources on planet Earth so each person could live like a king.

Paul recommend that Timothy advise the rich men of this world to put their trust not on riches, which are uncertain, but on the living God who gives us all things abundantly so we can enjoy them. (1 Timothy 6:17)

True riches are in God, not in the material goods, for all things with time are finished but our God remains forever. Wise Solomon said, "Honor the Lord with your possessions and with the first fruits of all your increase; so your barns will be filled with plenty, and your vats will overflow with new wine" (Proverbs 3:9-10).

1. ABEL'S OFFERING

God always makes sure that only He has first place in our heart. God didn't tell Cain and Abel what they were to offer, for this should be something spontaneous from their hearts. But with those offerings God was able to measure their level of commitment. Who was God pleased with as a result of their offering? The one who had a generous heart. But He rejected the one from the stingy, petty heart. "By faith Abel offered to God a more excellent sacrifice than Cain, through which he obtained witness that he was righteous, God testifying of his gifts; and through it he being dead still speaks," (Hebrews 11:4).

In this verse alone you can see which the steps for having a right offering are:

He offered

To offer is an act of our will. Through it we express
the gratitude we have for the person to whom it is
being offered. A great example of this can be seen in
children. When they have something they really like,
it's hard for them to share it with others. It's the age
where everyone revolves around themselves. But when
they are able to go through that stage in their lives
and have matured, it is easier to share with others
what they have.

God was pleased with Abel because he gave an offering
voluntarily to God, just like a child who knows how to
let go of what he loves.

Cain did what a child does who holds on to what he
most loves, giving away what he is not interested in.
That is why God did not receive Cain's offering gladly
but rather rejected it.

More excellent

Abel not only gave a good offering, he sought the best
one because he understood he should give the best to
God.

Normally, an excellent offering has a price. The better
the offering, the higher the cost. The man that wants
to give his wife a beautiful gem has to pay for it. The
man who wants to give the best to God, must be
willing to pay a price.

The Lord said, "And you shall love the Lord your God
with all your heart, with all your soul, with all your
mind, and with all your strength. This is the first
commandment," (Mark 12:30). A good offering is
a message of love where we combine our spiritual,
emotional and physical part into only one detail. And
when we give something to God, we don't do it waiting
to receive something for it but rather we're giving Him
our worship.

Sacrifice

Abel understood that the right offering implied sacrifice. Although he would have wanted to give himself to God, he looked for a substitute. And he chose the best of his flock to represent his complete surrender to God. The Lord Jesus said, "For God so loved the world that He gave his one and only Son, that whoever believed in him would not perish but have everlasting life," (John 3:16).
The way God showed his love towards the world was by sacrificing his only Son. When we give our best to God, we are somehow paying Him back for the offering of salvation that He gave us.

He was found to be righteous

As we saw before, an offering speaks. Abel's offering because the greatest testimony before God, a testimony showed him righteous.
When God tried Abraham and Abraham was willing to sacrifice his son, God was so pleased with this that he said to him, "By Myself I have sworn, because you have done this thing, and have not withheld your son, your only son; blessing I will bless you, and multiplying I will multiply your descendant as the stars of the heaven and as the sand which is on the seashore; and your descendant shall possess the gate of their enemies," (Genesis 22:16-17).

The offering speaks after death

Solomon said, "The memory of the righteous is blessed, but the name of the wicked will rot," (Proverbs 10:7).
The thing that immortalized Abel was the kind of offering he gave. If the offering we give God is so important, then we should make an effort to always give Him the best.

2. GOD TESTIFIES OF YOUR OFFERINGS

The offering becomes arguments in our favor. You may remember the incident of the centurion, whose servant was very sick in bed, and the elders of Israel defended him before Jesus, saying, "...the one for whom He should do this was deserving, for he loves our nation, and has built us a synagogue. Then Jesus went with them," (Luke 7:5-6). When Jesus heard about the offering he had given, he immediately went with them.

3. RICHES COME FROM GOD

David, referring to the great challenge and responsibility that his son Solomon had of building the house of God once he succeeded him on the throne, said, "Both riches and honor come from you, and you reign over all. In your hand is power and might; in your hand it is to make great and to give strength to all," (1 Chronicles 29:12).

When we understand that riches come from God and that only from Him all things proceed, we will be able to have a generous and giving heart towards Him. We will never give God something better than what He can give us.

"I know also my God, that You test the heart and have pleasure in uprightness. As for me, in the uprightness of my heart I have willingly offered all these things; and now with joy I have seen Your people, who are present here to offer willingly to You," (1 Chronicles 29:17).
David and the people of Israel had managed to gather abundant wealth for the construction of the temple of God, through the offerings the people had given voluntarily. With this prayer of David, we can see that:

God searches the hearts.
When Jesus came into the temple, the disciples were noticing how much people were offering externally.

Jesus was searching their hearts. Those that seemed to be very generous, the Lord identified stingy because they would give to God from their left overs. There was a woman who seemed to give very little, the Lord praised her because her offering was superior to that of because she made an effort to give it.

God is pleased with the righteous

Integrity is a result of generosity. Cain's selfishness destroyed him, and Judas' greed annihilated him. Men who touched God's heart were able to show their complete rendering to Him with their generosity. Abel's offering speaks even to this day; Abraham was willing to offer up his own son, and God was so pleased by this that He said, "By Myself I have sworn, because you have done this thing, and have not withheld your son, your only son; blessing I will bless you, and multiplying I will multiply your descendants as the stars of the heaven and as the sand which is on the seashore; and your descendants shall possess the gate of their enemies," (Genesis 22:16-17).

I have voluntarily offered all of this to you

Everything Solomon utilized for the construction of the temple-included gold, silver, the best wood and the best materials.
This came from the voluntary offerings of the people and from that which David had personally accumulated to give up for the building of the sanctuary. To do God's will implies a financial challenge. and these challenges can always be conquered as long as people have a good spirit to sow without interest and voluntarily.

The people have given to you spontaneously

The spontaneous offering is that which the people give deliberately, they give from their generosity.
"So let each one give as he purposes in his heart, not

grudgingly or of necessity; for God loves a cheerful giver. And God is able to make all grace abound toward you, that you, always having all sufficiency in all things, may have an abundance for every good work," (II Corinthians 9:7-8).

"The generous soul will be made rich; and he who waters will also be watered himself," (Proverbs 11:25).

LEARNING TO TITHE

For Israel it has always been very normal and habitual to separate the tenth part of their income for the work of God, even before God established it in the law of Moses. Abraham gave his tithes to Melchizedek and was blessed by him (Hebrews 7:2,6).

> "Then Jacob made a vow saying, If God will be with me, and keep me in this way that I am going, and give me bread to eat and clothing to put on, so that I come back to my father's house in peace, then the Lord shall be my God. And this stone which I have set as a pillar shall be God's house, and of all that You give me I will surely give a tenth to You," (Genesis 28:20-22).

> "Bring all the tithes to the storehouse, that there be food in my house, and try me now in this, says the Lord of hosts. If I will not open for you the windows of the heaven and pour out for you such blessing that there will not be room enough to receive it. And I will rebuke the devourer for your sakes, so that he will not destroy the fruit of your ground, nor shall the vine fail to bear fruit for you in the field; says the Lord of hosts. And all nations will call you blessed, for you will be a delightful land, says the Lord of hosts" (Malachi 3:10-12).

God prepared a series of blessings that will only be reached by those who have learned the importance of tithing:

- Bring all the tithes to the storehouse. The storehouse represents the church or the place where you are being spiritually edified. That is where you should take your tithes regularly.

- There is food in my house. Those that do the work of God are supported by the tithes. And God will recompense you because of it.

- Try me. This is the only text where God invites his children to try His faithfulness towards those that are obedient in giving. The Lord himself commits to opening the windows of heaven in response to our tithes and offerings and to pour out blessings upon us until they overflow. That is, more than what we can ask for or imagine.

- I will also rebuke the devourer for your sakes. The devourer is the spirit of ruin, the one that the Lord himself has made a commitment to separate us from it.

- And all nations will call you blessed. The blessing will be so clear that it will extend to other nations and they will see God's favor towards each of his children.

- You will be a delightful land. This happens only when the curse has been taken off and the blessing is restored to our territory.

CONCLUSION

The Lord tries the faithfulness of the heart according to what man offers to Him and He reciprocates.
Adam took of the fruit of the forbidden tree, which was a part of a finance belonging to God. Although the whole earth belonged to the first couple, their hearts turned away and they wanted more.

Of all the trees in the garden, God only reserved one for himself in order to try their faithfulness. Likewise, God has reserved ten percent of our income to try our commitment to Him.

APPLICATION

Suggest to your students that they chose to plant a seed or to make a commitment to the church, which will break the shortage of each family and ministry represented.

10 Questionnaire for further study

1. What is to offer?

_____

_____ .

2. Why was the Lord pleased with Abel's offering?

_____

_____ .

3. List the steps of a correct offering?

_____

_____ .

4. What does the Lord look at when a person gives an offering?

_____

_____ .

5. What is tithe?

_____

_____

_____ .

6. What benefits does tithing bring to your life?

_____

_____

_____ .

7. Be sincere with your self, and see what kind of attitude you have concerning tithes and offering. Ask God to forgive you if you have not been faithful to it or if your attitude has been incorrect. Make a covenant with Him that since today you will tithe and give offerings.